Methodological Individualism

Originating in the late 19th century and becoming the subject of ongoing methodological debates in the social sciences, methodological individualism is a paradigm that focuses on understanding social phenomena through the actions and choices of individuals rather than through collective explanations. This book highlights its theoretical bases as defined and developed in the writings of its founders and early proponents in the context of the liveliest methodological battles in the social sciences. It addresses fundamental epistemological issues, including the distinction between explanation in the social sciences and natural sciences, the rational bases for understanding social actions, the relation of social wholes to their parts, and the connections between social concepts and the phenomenal world. Bringing together new English translations of foundational texts by Carl Menger, Joseph Schumpeter, Georg Simmel, and Max Weber, this book provides key insights into one of the essential methodological paradigms in the social sciences, corrects misconceptions, and advances a deeper understanding of methodological individualism as a robust and valuable approach to explaining social phenomena. It will therefore appeal to scholars and students of sociology and sociological theory with an interest in questions of social science methodology.

Nathalie Bulle is a sociologist research director at the National Center for Scientific Research (CNRS, *Groupe d'Etude des Méthodes de l'Analyse Sociologique de la Sorbonne*) in France. Her interest in the analysis of human thought, in its common or scientific form, is at the core of her work applied to educational ideas and the epistemology of the social sciences. She has published articles on methodological individualism in the *Philosophy of the Social Sciences*, the *Journal of Classical Sociology*, and *L'Année sociologique*. She is currently co-editing the *Palgrave Handbook of Methodological Individualism* (with Francesco Di Iorio). http://www.nathaliebulle.com/

Routledge Studies in Social and Political Thought

This series explores core issues in political philosophy and social theory. Addressing theoretical subjects of both historical and contemporary relevance, the series has broad appeal across the social sciences. Contributions include new studies of major thinkers, key debates, and critical concepts. The full series can be viewed here.

Cultural Capital and Creative Communication
(Anti-)Modern and (Non-)Eurocentric Perspective
Oana Șerban

Regimes of Capital in the Post-Digital Age
Edited by Szymon Wróbel and Krzysztof Skonieczny

The Not So Outrageous Idea of a Christian Sociology
Joseph Scimecca

Against the Background of Social Reality
Defaults, Commonplaces, and the Sociology of the Unmarked
Carmelo Lombardo and Lorenzo Sabetta

The Cognitive Foundations of Classical Sociological Theory
Ryan McVeigh

Social Theory and the Political Imaginary
Practice, Critique, and History
Craig Browne

Being a Lived Body
From a Neo-phenomenological Point of View
Tonino Griffero

Revisiting Social Theory
Challenges and Possibilities
Edited by D.V. Kumar

Methodological Individualism

Introduction and Founding Texts

Nathalie Bulle

Routledge
Taylor & Francis Group

LONDON AND NEW YORK

First published in 2024
by Routledge
4 Park Square, Milton Park, Abingdon, Oxon, OX14 4RN

and by Routledge
605 Third Avenue, New York, NY 10158

Routledge is an imprint of the Taylor & Francis Group, an informa business

British Library Cataloguing-in-Publication Data
A catalogue record for this book is available from the British Library

ISBN: 9781032582801 (hbk)
ISBN: 9781032627038 (pbk)
ISBN: 9781032627021 (ebk)

DOI: 10.4324/9781032627021

Typeset in Times New Roman
by Deanta Global Publishing Services, Chennai, India

To the masters with whom I learned to read the great texts before discussing sociology:

Raymond Boudon, Mohamed Cherkaoui, Bernard Valade, François Chazel, and Jean Baechler

Contents

1 The turmoiled emergence of methodological individualism within the social sciences landscape

A path to its understanding

1.1 The emergence of Methodological Individualism and its opposition to Historicism

According to certain interpretations of methodological individualism, the core truth it contains is banal and lacks methodological implication, namely that the only acting entities in the social sciences are individuals. Alongside this interpretation, there is a second one which argues that MI is a methodologically untenable reductionist approach that would require the properties of individuals to be independent of social wholes, in order to "reduce" processes involving the social wholes to processes involving only individuals. On these grounds, many philosophers have expended considerable effort in demonstrating its alleged conceptual inconsistencies, without regard to the fact that prominent sociologists, economists, and philosophers have attached their names to it, resolutely for the sake of science.

The disagreements between proponents of MI and its detractors have animated the liveliest methodological disputes in the social sciences for almost a century and a half. Any attempt to overcome them by superficial compromises would amount to disregarding the possible incompatibilities underlying these recurrent conflicts. It is indeed significant that the proponents of MI, who are among the founding figures of the social sciences, have contributed to clarifying its theoretical foundations in the context of these methodological battles, which keep reappearing in barely renewed forms.

The premises of MI were first developed by the economist Carl Menger (before the term itself came into use) in a memorable "battle of methods" (*Methodenstreit*) that pitted him against Gustav Schmoller, a prominent figure of the German Historical School belonging to the current known as "Historicism." Menger's publication in 1883 of his book *Investigations into the Method of the Social Science with Special Reference to Economics* [*Untersuchungen uber die Methode der Socialwissenschaften und der Politschen Oekonomie insbesondere*], in which he defended a theoretical approach to the social sciences that laid some of the essential foundations of methodological individualism, against the empirical realism of the Historical School, provoked a sharp criticism from Schmoller in the same year, *On the*

DOI: 10.4324/9781032627021-1

Methodology of Political and Social Sciences [*Zur Methodologie der Staats- und Sozialwissenschaften*] in a journal called *Yearbook for Legislation, Administration and Economics* [*Jahrbuch für Gesetzgebung, Verwaltung und Volkswirtsch*], to which Menger replied in 1884 in the form of a series of 16 letters with the evocative title *The Errors of Historicism in German Economics* [*Die Irrtümer des Historismus in der Deutschen Nationalökonomie*]. Furthermore, Georg Simmel's methodological work *The Problems of the Philosophy of History* [*Die Probleme der Geschichtsphilosophie*] (Simmel, 1907/1905), which develops the "understanding" foundations of the indi- vidualist methodology for the social sciences, presents itself as a criticism of historicism, in which "individualities dissolved into history, which is the history of the mind," claiming that "the liberation that Kant achieved from naturalism is also needed from historicism."[1] In this work, Simmel opposes, in particular, the historicist methodology of the renowned historian Leopold von Ranke, and points out the contradictions of the historicism of the Marxian theory, which claims to be materialist and in practice relies on the psychologi- cal springs of history involving individual aspirations. But this does not stop there. Max Weber, often considered the "father" of methodological individu- alism in sociology, who provided his basic conceptual categories and refined his methodological principles, developed his epistemological reflections in the context of a critical examination of Wilhelm Roscher and Karl Knie's his- toricist approaches to political economy: *Roscher and Knies and the Logical Problems of Historical Economics* [*Roscher und Knies und die logischen Probleme der historischen Nationalökonomie*] (Weber, 1903–1906). Joseph Schumpeter, who made the expression "methodological individualism" offi- cial in a chapter of his first book, *The Nature and Essence of Economic Theory* [*Das Wesen und der Hauptinhalt der theoretischen Nationalökonomie*], pub- lished in 1908, links MI to the "new system" in economics, which is rooted in Menger's work, and places it in the context of the ongoing methodological dispute. A few decades later, the term MI gained popularity on the occasion of a notable revival of the battle waged by the proponents of MI against the vari- ous forms of historicism still developed in the social sciences, as evidenced in the articles published between 1942 and 1945 by Friedrich Hayek (1942, 1943, 1944) and Karl Popper (1944a, 1944b, 1945) in the journal *Economica*, which were respectively collected in Hayek's *Counter Revolution of Science* (1955) and Popper's *The Poverty of Historicism* (1957). Hayek directs his criticism of "scientism" in the social sciences along with closely correlated forms of "objectivism," "collectivism," and "historicism," while Popper dedi- cates his own criticism of historicism to the "memory of the countless men, women and children of all creeds or nations or races who fell victims to the fascist and communist belief in Inexorable Laws of Historical Destiny."

In light of these events, it appears that the theoretical foundations of meth- odological individualism were developed in opposition to the same enemy. This fact is not insignificant for understanding its meaning, even if this enemy seems somewhat distant today, to the extent that one might wonder whether discussing it is not simply an archaeological exercise, albeit an important one, but disconnected from the contemporary landscape of the social sciences. Readers will assess for themselves. Gaining an understanding of historicism and, based on that, comprehending the epistemological and methodological principles opposed by advocates of MI, can be highly instructive.

1.2 The empiricist and materialist foundations of historicism and the naturalization of the human subject

Historicism represents the dominant approach to historical, economic, and social phenomena that developed in the 19th century under various doctrinal forms, drawing inspiration from perspectives as diverse as those associated with the names of Friedrich Hegel, Auguste Comte, Karl Marx, and Herbert Spencer. Historicism reflects the dominant influence of the concept of evolution during this period. This influence pervaded in two main ways, both of which converged in the conception of human beings as evolving products of their natural and social environments. First, this approach was inspired by the significant advances in evolutionary biology and, second, by the overthrow of Hegelian idealism by Marx and Engels. In this regard, Hannah Arendt (1958, p. 116) observes the coincidence between the biological model of evolution from the lower forms of life to its most elaborate forms, and the historical development of humanity as a whole in Marx's thought, a coincidence marked by the use of the concept of process. Historicist currents share a tendency to view social science phenomena as part of a global process of development, so their explanation requires situating them in the context of a current of history. This is reflected in the definition of historicism proposed by Maurice Mandelbaum (1971, p. 42), in his *Study in Nineteenth-Century Thought*, as "the belief that an adequate understanding of the nature of any phenomenon and an adequate assessment of its value are to be gained through considering it in terms of the place which it occupied and the role which it played within a process of development." The idea of evolution and their empiricist orientation lead historicists to prioritize the accumulation of facts over theoretical presuppositions that isolate elements and fix their meaning, whereas all elements are assumed to be intrinsically interconnected and subject to overall change. According to historicism, understanding past events, human actions, and works requires a meticulous study of the specific historical contexts, mores, places, and circumstances of their historical process of emergence.

Historicist approaches have two major consequences for social science research. First, they direct scientific inquiry toward the search for laws governing historical development, which are seen as relative and provisional. Second, these approaches tend to conceive of the basic characteristics of the human subject as inherently variable. In particular, historicism shares similarities with evolutionary theories in biology, which emphasize the phylogenetic perspective applied to genetic changes in animal or plant species and extended to humans. These ideas are also reflected in organicism, which rose to prominence in the 19th century in close association with historicism. Organicism posits that the effects of cultural models on individuals determine changes in the basic attributes of human characteristics within a population, changes that were often conceived at the time as potentially interfering with the genetic heritage of that population.[2]

Friedrich Hayek pointed out the connection between historicism and the belief in the variability of the human mind, attributing it to the scientistic empiricist prejudices:

> The whole idea of the variability of the human mind is a direct result of the erroneous belief that mind is an object which we observe as we observe physical facts. The sole difference, however, between mind and physical objects, which entitles us to speak of mind at all, is precisely that wherever we speak of mind we interpret what we observe in terms of categories which we know only because they are the categories in which our own mind runs.
>
> (Hayek, 1943, p. 62)

This is consistent with the idea that the concept of causality in the dominant forms of historicism at the time is akin to Humean causality, which connects observable elements through a principle of uniformity in succession, and thus through links whose validity is essentially contextual (Bostaph, 1978). This interpretation can be supplemented by the connections between historicism and the materialistic naturalism of the 19th century. The associationist psychology that inspires Humean empiricism suggests that all ideas are derived from sensory impressions that the mind associates with each other in the course of its experience of the external world. Although the metaphor is debatable, it has been called "mental atomism" because the links between its basic elements (elementary sensations) are "external" in the sense that they involve no intrinsic interpretive dimension, and its laws have been analogously compared to those governing the physical world, thus paving the way for materialist or physicalist reductionism.

In various texts, Raymond Boudon notes that the variants of historicism share the assumption that human behavior is determined by material causes, whether they take social, psychological, or biological paths, they escape the control of human consciousness. Imitating the natural sciences, which have succeeded in replacing explanations based on final causes with explanations based on material causes, such as Darwin's theory of evolution, the social and human sciences have tended to naturalize the human subject by conceiving of him "as the point of application of material forces" (Boudon, 2008, p. 43). This implies that the principles of behavior, values, and beliefs of social actors should be explained by their immersion in their social environments of birth and life, and thus determined by irrational factors. These ideas shed light on the underlying principles of historicism, which were later taken up in various forms of "culturalism" or "sociologism."

1.3 The opposition between Menger's individualist method and Schmoller's historicism within the *Methodenstreit*

It was in the intellectual context of naturalism, empiricism, and material-ism, in the sense mentioned above, that the "battle of methods" took place, which led to the conceptualization of the individualist method against the prevailing historicist approaches of the time. This battle pitted Carl Menger, the founder of the Austrian school of economics, against Gustav Schmoller, the leader of the historical school of political economy. The stakes of this confrontation can hardly be measured without considering the conceptions of the two protagonists, which unfortunately are not equally accessible to the public. Only a handful of Schmoller's articles have been translated into English. The reason given for this is the language barrier (Peukert, 2001), but it is far from being the most important one, knowing that his works are gener-ally only available in German Gothic. However, the translation of his *Layout of General Economics* [*Grundriss der allgemeinen Volkswirtschaftslehre*] (Schmoller, 1900/1905–1908) into French, which corresponds to a course in general political economy that Schmoller taught for thirty-six years, provides access to his thought, especially his conception of political economy as a "real whole," that is, as:

a coherent whole, whose living parts react on each other and in which the Whole, as such, has certain effects; a whole which notwithstanding the eternal change of the parts and its own change, remains the same in its individual features for years and decades; which, insofar as it changes, appears as a body in the process of developing.

(Schmoller, 1900/1905, p. 16)

In this vast treatise, Schmoller paints a general picture of the social and eco-nomic evolution of peoples, involving his holistic (in the causal sense) con-ception of social development, in which the social wholes direct the action of their parts, so the parts follow logics defined at the level of the wholes:

The national economy is the system of economic and social habits and arrangements of the people, considered and acting as a whole, dominated by the spirit of this people, which is one and always the same, and by identical material causes.

(Schmoller, 1900/1905, p. 19)

Because:

> Men living under the same conditions, belonging to the same race, the same people, the same locality, and subject to the same causes, and the same influences, in spite of differences of little importance in detail, present the same principal traits, similar qualities of body and mind.
>
> (Schmoller, 1900/1905, p. 42)

Thus, Schmoller proposes to uncover the distinctive characteristics "of each race and each people," which he conceives as "physiological and psychological units, based on the community of blood and spirit" (Schmoller, 1900/1905, p. 338). He even goes so far as to praise the author of *An Essay on the Inequality of the Human Races* [*Essai sur l'inégalité des races humaines* (1853–1855)], Arthur de Gobineau, for having "proved" the significance of race, while tempering some of the excesses of Gobineau's primarily genetic interpretation of the progress or regression of peoples. Schmoller's perspective is influenced by Spencerian ideas, and he believes in the heredity of repeated experiences, so his causally holistic view of historical evolution brings into play two large groups of factors that reinforce each other to account for the homogeneity of the behavior of individuals within the same people: environmental and natural determinants. Environmental determinants would act through social institutions, relying on imitation, education, and social contacts, and would tend to become physiologically anchored in the organism over time and to combine with natural determinants (Schmoller, 1900/1905, p. 353), so that this evolutionary process is likened to the development of an organism. On this basis, Schmoller formulates generalities about the evolution of peoples and discusses the potentially harmful consequences of their mixtures, which will not be elaborated here for the contemporary reader.

It is difficult to comprehend the general praise that Schmoller's work received, being heralded as "an event of first rank in the history of the economic literature" of the year (*Journal of Political Economy*), likely to attract the interest of students of economics, like "ANY book of Professor Schmoller" (*The Economic Journal*). Schmoller has even been described as "among the most human of German economists" whose writings give the impression that his interest in "problems" is incidental to his interest in people (*American Journal of Sociology*). Was it possible that his historicist theses and their implications were not challenged at the time? A hint of reservation seems to come from the notion that "although he evidently tries to be impartial, some of his criticisms on [other] races, including the unfortunate Yankees, would be laughable if they were not so brilliantly written" (*Political Science Quarterly*). It is interesting to refer on this subject to Weber (1922, Chap. 1), who is particularly doubtful, clearly with reference to historicist theses, about the role played by the genetic inheritance of "races" on sociologically relevant behavior.[3]

In his posthumous *History of Economic Reasoning*, Karl Pribram (1983, p. 372) states unequivocally that after World War I, organismic reasoning provided the logical foundation for extreme nationalism in German universities and that "the numerical preponderance of those teachers who had been educated in the methodological principles adopted by Gustav Schmoller's school was incontestable [and] prepared the soil — for the most part unwittingly — for the subsequent acceptance of the National Socialist creed."

Certainly, in his struggle against Schmoller, Menger was far from having grasped the full extent of the socio-political dangers of historicist thinking, which, unfortunately, the history of the 20th century has experienced. For his part, Schmoller, as Pribram (1983, p. 50) explains, failed to recognize the fundamental logical problems at the heart of the controversy. He attempted to reduce them to an opposition between inductive and deductive methods, claiming that he had already surpassed it with his own method — an argument widely echoed by his followers — although he did not address the issues raised by Menger's approach. These were profound forms of incompatibility, as Samuel Bostaph (1978) has argued.

Menger, in his response to Schmoller's criticism of his *Investigations*, states that the objections and attacks he faces provide him with an opportunity to clarify his ideas for an informed audience. To start, let us note two of his remarks that illuminate the scientific contours of the individualist method he advocates. The first comment concerns the definition of the specific subject matter of the social sciences, namely the understanding of individual phenomena in their collective dimension:

> The task of the social sciences is in fact to present the individual phenomena of human life from the point of view of a collective observation, each phenomenon having, however, significance only insofar as it is important for the collective image of human life in itself.
>
> (Menger, 1884/1935, p. 76)

The second comment concerns the politicization of the debate by Schmoller, who accuses Menger of advocating Manchesterism.[4] Menger (1884/1935, pp. 82–84) explains in this regard that not only is this presumption completely unfounded and lacking any support in his work (as nothing is "more remote in his thought than the service of the interests of capitalism"), but also that Manchesterism has "as much to do with the question of the propriety of an exact theory of economics as a gunpowder conspiracy has with the question of the propriety of theoretical chemistry." These points tend to counter both the reductionist (or "atomistic") prejudice that individuals in methodological individualism should have properties essentially independent of social wholes

– though this needs further clarification – and the prejudice of its association with political individualism.

1.4 Menger and the compositive method in the social sciences

Menger's theoretical approach assumes a process of isolation that is twofold. First, isolation involves the abstraction of the essential elements of a phenomenon from the other "accidental" elements of empirical reality. Second, isolation involves the construction of a (closed) theoretical system within the framework of the implementation of exact laws (this idea of exact laws is challenged by Weber). Menger describes his "compositive" method as follows:

> It is a question of reducing the real phenomena of the national economy to their simplest and most typical elements and of explaining to us, on the basis of the method of isolation, the (exact) laws of the market economy, according to which the complex phenomena of the economy emerge from these elements, in order to enable us, by this means, to understand, not the social phenomena "in their full empirical reality", but certainly their economic dimension.
>
> (Menger, 1884/1935, p. 19)

On this basis, according to Menger, the "exact" orientation of theoretical research should follow an approach analogous to that of the natural sciences, but "different." Menger explains that the success of the natural sciences is not only due to the observation of external regularities in the relationships between phenomena (empirical laws), but rather to the "search for internal regularities" allowing complex phenomena to be understood as a "fabric of internal laws" (Menger, 1884/1935, p. 127). He further notes that this orientation of theoretical research is universal in science and does not deny the unity of organic wholes, so that the parts involved are not a priori supposed to be independent of the wholes to which they belong. Moreover, he suggests that the compositive method is based on a characteristic disposition of the human mind in the construction of knowledge.[5] What, then, is the specificity of the social sciences compared to the natural sciences in this respect? Menger refers several times to the "principles of rational action in the field of national economy," but it is interesting to cite one passage of his *Investigations* on this subject:

> The ultimate elements upon which the exact theoretical interpretation of natural phenomena must rest are "atoms" and "forces." Both are of a non-empirical nature. We cannot represent the "atoms" at all, nor the forces of nature other than by an image, and in reality, we only understand them as causes of real movements that are unknown to us. This results in quite

extraordinary difficulties for the exact interpretation of natural phenomena. The situation is different in the exact social sciences. Here, the ultimate elements of our analysis are human individuals and their aspirations, which are of empirical nature, giving the exact theoretical social sciences a significant advantage over the exact natural sciences. The "limits of the knowledge of nature" and the resulting difficulties for the theoretical understanding of natural phenomena do not really exist for the exact research in the realm of social sciences. When A[uguste] Comte conceives "societies" as real organisms, and even as organisms of a more complex nature than natural organisms, and when he designates their theoretical interpretation as an incomparably more complicated and challenging scientific problem, he commits a serious error. His theory would only be acknowledged by social scientists who, given the current state of the theoretical natural sciences, would have the quite foolish idea of wanting to interpret the phenomena of society not in a specifically social-scientific way but rather in a atomistic-scientific way proper to the natural sciences.
(Menger, 1883, note pp. 157–158)

Weber emphasized Menger's contribution to the specificity of the basic units of the social sciences and the advantage these sciences have over the natural sciences:

In the domain of the sciences of society, we are in the fortunate position of [being able to] observe the internal structure of 'smallest elements' of which society is composed and which must permeate the whole web of its relations. Menger was the first, followed by many others, to make this point.
(Weber, 1903–1906/1975, note p. 24)

The social-scientific approach, in contrast to the atomistic scientific approach, brings into play individual aspirations as understandable driving forces and their potentially unintended social outcomes as major sources of social change. This is why, in his *Investigations*, Menger emphasizes the unintentional origin of institutions (language, religion, state, law, money, markets, etc.) and other social structures and phenomena of particular interest to the social sciences. He describes this origin as "organic," in contrast to the "pragmatic" and "unhistorical" origin based on agreements or legislation. He notes, however, that some thinkers simply call it "organic" without resolving anything. According to Menger, the compositive method is essential to explaining the "organic" development process, that is, unintentionally created, of these social structures:

Language, religion, law, even the state itself, and, to mention more specifically some social phenomena of an economic nature, the phenomena of markets, competition, money, and many other social formations already appear to us in historical epochs when there can be no question of their having been founded voluntarily by a deliberate activity of the communities as such or their leaders. We are dealing here with the emergence of social institutions which largely serve the welfare of society, often even vitally so, and yet are not the result of the social activity of the community. Here is the curious, perhaps the most curious, problem of the social sciences: *How is it that institutions which serve the common good and are of great importance for its development can come into being without a **common** will to create them?* [...] The theoretical understanding of the nature and development of these phenomena can therefore only be achieved in the same way as for the aforementioned social formations, namely by tracing back to their elements, that is, to the individual factors that caused them, and by studying the laws according to which the complex phenomena of human economy in question develop from these elements.

(Menger, 1883, pp. 163, 182)

The individualist method developed by Menger thus brings into play the aspirations and choices of social actors and the effects of the combination of actions and interactions, with the aim of providing a relevant explanation of the evolution over time of social structures that play a supra-individual role, often different from the intentions that gave rise to them, especially in the service of the common good.

1.5 Schumpeter's defense of methodological individualism in economics

After Menger, it is worth noting the role played by Schumpeter in the history of methodological individualism within economic thought. In his first book, published in 1908, Schumpeter notoriously formalized the expression, although he later developed his economic thought on other grounds. As Hayek writes in his preface to a later edition of Schumpeter's chapter on MI in that book:

In 1908, when Joseph Schumpeter at the age of twenty-five, published his "Wesen und Hauptinhalt der theoretischen National ekonomie" (*Essence and Chief Contents of Economic Theory*), it attracted much attention, with the brilliance of its exposition. Moreover, though he had been trained at the University of Vienna and had been a leading member of the famous seminar of Eugen von Boehm- Bawerk, he had also absorbed the teaching of Leon Walras, who had received little notice by the Austrians and had adopted the positivist approach to science expounded by the Austrian physicist Ernst Mach. In the course of time he moved further away from the characteristic tenets of the Austrian school so that it became increasingly doubtful later whether he could still be counted as a member of that group (...) Though the author may later no longer have been prepared to defend the ideas of his first work, they are certainly essential enough to the understanding of the development of economic theory. Indeed Schumpeter made a contribution to the tradition of the Austrian School which is sufficiently original to be made available to a wider public.

(Hayek, 1980, p. 1)

Schumpeter's book helps illuminate where MI stood at the turn of the 20th century and vigorously challenges the confusions that fuel criticisms of the individualist method, especially those of a political and moral nature. First, Schumpeter emphasizes the outdated yet pervasive character of classical theory (represented by Adam Smith, David Ricardo, and their immediate successors) in economics. He notes that classical theory provided the conceptual underpinnings both for its direct critics, from the Historical School, and for those who renewed economics with the conceptions of the Marginalist School (represented by Carl Menger, Stanley Jevons, and Léon Walras). Despite this legacy, Schumpeter explains that the system of modern theory is essentially new compared to the classical system, not only in terms of assumptions and method, but also in spirit. In particular, he asserts that the individualist method that characterizes the new system of economics is inherently free from political bias. Following Menger, Schumpeter defends that it is impossible to derive from the individualist method an argument for or against political individualism, and that political individualism and methodological individualism "have absolutely nothing in common."

In light of the above, it is interesting here to examine more closely the position of MI in relation to classical economics.

Some analyses originating from the classical system have de facto convergences with MI, as in the case of Adam Smith's invisible hand, which reflects the social importance of the unintended consequences of rational individual actions. However, one cannot conclude that there is a general convergence in principle. The case of John Stuart Mill, with his empiricist orientation, reveals the complexity of the relationships involved. In fact, Mill's reductionist psychological assumptions imply the causal role that historicist approaches ascribe to collective concepts such as the "spirit of the people," which MI fundamentally opposes:

There is, however, among these separate departments one which cannot be passed over in silence, being of a more comprehensive and commanding character than any of the other branches into which the social science may admit of being divided. Like them, it is directly conversant with the causes of only one class of social facts, but a class which exercises, immediately or remotely, a paramount influence over the rest. I allude to what may be termed Political Ethology,[6] or the theory of the causes which determine the type of character belonging to a people or to an age. Of all the subordinate branches of the social science this is the most completely in its infancy [...] Yet to whoever well considers the matter, it must appear that the laws of national (or collective) character are by far the most important class of sociological laws.

(Mill, 1843, Chap. 9 § 4)

Mill's hypotheses also support the kind of historicist research into the provisional laws of historical development:

All phenomena of society are phenomena of human nature, generated by the action of outward circumstances upon masses of human beings; and if, therefore, the phenomena of human thought, feeling, and action are subject to fixed laws, the phenomena of society cannot but conform to fixed laws, the consequence of the preceding.

(Mill, 1843, Chap. 6 § 2)

Mill's reductionism is rooted in a metaphysical (and not methodological!) individualism in which individuals are metaphysically unchanged, whether they are social beings or not (see Thilly, 1923). This conception is related to the psychologism underlying his historicism, which involves "an abstract, atomic, mechanical, deterministic conception of the human mind, the human individual, human society and human history" (Thilly 1923, p. 4). Equipped with the laws of associationist psychology and through interaction with their environment, human beings develop collective behaviors that are supposed to underlie the main sociological laws. Popper (1945/1966) pointed out that Mill's psychologism forces him to use historicist methods that are incompatible with methodological individualism, where reference to human reason and the subjective meaning of action presupposes a social learning:

It [the psychologistic version of historicism] is a desperate position because this theory of a pre-social human nature which explains the foundation of society — a psychologistic version of the 'social contract' — is not only an historical myth, but also, as it were, a methodological myth. It can hardly be seriously discussed, for we have every reason to believe that man or rather his ancestor was social prior to being human (considering, for example, that language presupposes society). But this implies that social institutions, and with them, typical social regularities or sociological laws, must have existed prior to what some people are pleased to call 'human nature', and to human psychology. If a reduction is to be attempted at all, it would therefore be more hopeful to attempt a reduction or interpretation of psychology in terms of sociology than the other way round.

(Popper, 1945/1966, p. 304)

Schumpeter does not fail to express his skepticism about Mill. Nevertheless, he does not elaborate much on what the individualist method means. In fact, he mistakenly equates MI with its practical applications in economics and obscures its wider significance for the social sciences as a whole. For example, in upholding the pragmatic goals of the individualist method as he could observe it, that is, in asserting that the individualist method is intended to lead "briefly and opportunely" to results that are broadly useful, Schumpeter overlooks the deeper epistemological perspective developed by Menger. In particular, Menger (1883, p. 88) considers the reference, in the theoretical elaboration, to the parts of a complex phenomenon as an effort to highlight the "coworking [*Zusammenwirkens*] of the factors of its origin." And while Weber emphasizes the fundamental distinction between model and reality, he also believes that the model can serve its heuristic function of identifying real causes only by capturing certain essential elements of the action in question:

> Without evidence that an individual's behavior actually occurs to some extent as we assume, such a "law," [Gresham law in Economics] however apparently accurate, would be a worthless construct for understanding actual action.
>
> (Weber, 1922, p. 5)

Thus, Schumpeter's view of MI also differs from that of Weber, whose ideas he would have been familiar with.[7] Schumpeter was undoubtedly aware of the limitations of modeling individual decision-making processes according to the norms of strictly rational teleological action, as usually used in economics. This may explain why he attributed a purely pragmatic value to the individualist method based on its applications in this field. But his pragmatism also seems intent on dispelling a false metaphysical alternative, namely whether society or the individual is ultimately the "driving" force behind social phenomena. Schumpeter is right to reject metaphysical debates on this subject in economics, but wrong to transfer them to sociology. The alternative simply does not make sense for MI, which sees the individual as a social actor from the outset and, in this respect, regards the social whole and its individual parts as relative entities, evacuating the question of priority as a misconception. The rejection of such a priority does not preclude the pursuit of causal realism, which, as Weber explains, involves seeking genuine causal relations that include actors' reasons for acting, as we shall see.

The development of the epistemological foundations of MI by figures such as Simmel and Weber has broadened its scope, clarified sociology's contribution, and strengthened its explanatory ambition.

1.6 Simmel's understanding approach and the mental nature of history

With Simmel and Weber, the role of human rationality in MI becomes clearer, moving from a principle involving de facto normative schemes in economic models to a methodological principle involving the general human capacity to attribute meaning to things and, therefore, to act in accordance with that meaning. The consideration of rationality as a human capacity based on the content of consciousness makes MI an intrinsically "understanding" approach. In his introduction to *Economy and Society*, Weber explicitly refers the reader to Simmel's discussions of this topic in *Problems of the Philosophy of History* [*Problemen der Geschichtsphilosophie*].

Simmel's book[8] mentioned by Weber, which, according to its subtitle, is presented as a "study of epistemology," explicitly draws on a neo-Kantian conception of human knowledge, and thus involves the question of the construction of meaning and understanding. In this regard, Simmel points out that Kant, with his strict separation of the a priori from the empirical, failed to fully grasp the extent of the a priori forms of knowledge that shape our experience.

Before turning to Simmel's reflections in *Problems*, it is worth mentioning the role that the concept of social forms plays in his work. This role is the subject of an article published in French in the journal *L'Année sociologique*: "Comment les formes sociales se maintiennent? [How social forms are maintained?]" (Simmel, 1896/1897). Simmel recognizes the sui generis reality of the unity of society, whose mode of preservation has nothing in common with that of human beings. This recognition could lead to the idea that society is an autonomous reality with its own laws, leading a life independent of its members. Simmel refers to examples such as "language, the church, law, political and social organization," which are elements of what Popper would later call the "World 3" — the world of the products of the human mind.[9] These social forms, which involve all individuals but no one in particular, justify the idea of the organic origin of "unintentionally created" social phenomena previously evoked by Menger. In a sense, they dominate the individuals and do not depend on the same conditions as individual life. However, as Simmel explains, the products of the human mind in question are of a mental nature and have no reality outside the personal intelligences. How, then, can we explain this supra-individual nature of collective phenomena, the objectivity and relative autonomy of social forms? Simmel's answer is that we must admit that there are only individuals and that all phenomena seeming to constitute an independent reality above them are actually resolved in their reciprocal actions. But, in order to achieve our goals of knowledge, we must interpret the relations established between human beings with the help of conceptual constructs. Therefore, it is only through a process of method, as Simmel specifies, that we speak of the state, law, fashion, etc., but:

> just as the biologist has been able to replace the vital force, which seemed to hover above the various organs, by the understanding of their recipro-cal action, the sociologist, in his turn, must strive to uncover the specific processes that actually give rise to social phenomena, at whatever distance he must remain from his ideal.
>
> (Simmel 1896/1897, p. 75)

In order to maintain itself, the group seems to manifest an autonomous power of resistance, an enduring unity that transcends the limits of space and time. Simmel attributes this apparent causal power to the mental nature of the a priori forms that constitute groups in depth and which, unlike the material pro-cesses of the natural sciences, can be transmitted between individuals (if we leave aside genetic inheritance, he specifies, which does not apply to groups without physiological bonds, such as the Catholic clergy). These forms are implicitly transmitted as interpretive premises in the course of social interac-tions, and are maintained by the essentially gradual renewal of the group, so that the mental bonds they represent are maintained over time in a supra-indi-vidual manner. The very concept of social form reflects the institutionaliza-tion of a certain way of understanding the world, involving the socially shared character of the vectors of meaning, or "a priori," that these forms represent.

These few elements shed light on Boudon's later assertion that one can-not fully understand the Simmelian notion of form — which implies the interpretive dimension of human thought — without seeing that this feature of Simmel's theory of explanation "is organically linked to the postulate of methodological individualism" (Boudon, 1984, p. 12).

In *The Problems*, Simmel explains that the essence of history is mental. In this regard, he opposes the methods of historicism that seek to exhaust the understanding of phenomena from the observable elements of the context in which they are embedded:

> It has been argued that in order to understand Kant, it is necessary to deduce him historically. But if it were impossible to grasp the content of the pre-Kantian doctrines and their relation to Kant's work from a logical and psychological point of view, if this relation did not constitute a series that could be understood independently of its historical realiza-tion, then the historical succession between the earlier philosophers and Kant would correspond to the discontinuity of mere moments in time [...] the elements of this series [syllogism] also constitute a temporal

sequence, but they would have no unity if there were not a timeless connection of meaning between them, indifferent to all that precedes and
follows. [...] Historicism, because of its empiricist orientation, believes
that it can derive this unity from "historical reality" itself. On the contrary, we must perceive this unity in order for reality to appear historical
to us at all.

(Simmel, 1892/1907, note p. 35)

According to Simmel, all processes related to the historical approach, even
those related to material phenomena such as the construction of a tunnel, interest it only insofar as they represent mental events, but in a completely different sense from that usually understood in psychology. The historical approach
is based on an "abstract" psychology applied to the contents of consciousness, which holds a psychological hypothesis to be true only if it describes a
mechanism that we think we understand. The epistemological question then
concerns the meaning and conditions of this "understanding." Simmel argues
that it is based on a fundamental operation: the ability to subsume observable human actions "under the categories of invisible purposes and feelings
which are necessary to bring these actions into an understandable context"
(Simmel, 1907/1905, p. 18). In order to achieve this, it is necessary to be able
to represent the meaningful mental processes that underlie these actions. This
objectification relies on an operation of reconstruction that implies a principle
of rationality and involves a series of mediating elements such as externalizations, transpositions, symbolizations, etc. In this respect, understanding elimi-
nates any form of psychic determinism and instead recognizes the meaningful
development of states of consciousness, knowing that all elements belong to
the same individual unit:

From an epistemological standpoint, the link that unites the various features of a historical subject, and transforms the complexes of representations accompanying a historical action into a meaningful unity, is different
from a cause or a reason. It is neither the empirical law of the event nor the
formal law of the content, but a third of its own: meaning.

(Simmel, 1907/1905, p. 50)

The semantic context of historical understanding implies bringing into play
the social forms mentioned above, which underlie the very possibility of this
understanding.

It is noteworthy that despite the centrality of mental elements in these conceptions, Simmel's sociology does not overestimate the role of consciousness.
As he explains, there is a blurred boundary between the unconscious and the
conscious, because consciousness is progressively excluded from behavior

once it becomes habitual and mechanical. But the continuity between the conscious and the unconscious allows us to refer to the meaning of the action involved, as long as it is understood that the latter may remain implicit for the subject. This is why, in the theoretical interpretation, the distinction between conscious and unconscious reveals the impact of personal choice, with recourse to the unconscious tending to indicate our ignorance of the potential conscious motivations.

Simmel's understanding approach is supported by Weber, who states that "by far the most elaborate attempt, from the point of view of logic, to formulate a theory of 'understanding' is to be found in the second edition of Simmel's *Philosophy of History* (pp. 27–62)" (Weber, 1903–1906/1975, p. 59), even though Weber appears to be critical of Simmel on various occasions, including in his *Roscher & Knies*, where he expresses reservations, stating that the aim of interpretation is not to reproduce the mental state of the subjects but to gain "causal knowledge" (Weber, 1903–1906/1975, p. 61).

1.7 Sociological explanation according to Weber and meaningful purposeful actions

As we have seen, Weber owes certain methodological principles of MI to Menger, and certain implications of the understanding method underlying the individualist method to Simmel.

Weber's epistemological reflection, especially developed in his analysis of the *Logical Problems of Historical Economics* in Roscher & Knies (Weber, 1903–1906/1975), benefits from Menger's work but corrects, or rather deepens, his explanatory model by highlighting the specific source of the intelligibility of phenomena in the social sciences, associated with the idea of understanding. Weber explains that in Roscher's work, the impossibility in principle of explaining social wholes as causally deriving from individual phenomena, the latter being conceived as organic not only analogically but properly metaphysically, is a dogma of the doctrine that is therefore unquestionable and not subject to justification. On the contrary, Weber argues, we have the capacity to acquire knowledge of the internal characteristics of the elementary units of society – units which are the vectors of all the relations that structure it. This capacity does not concern psychology at all, because if this science develops an approach that tends to reduce intellectual and mental activity to natural processes, it is of no more interest to the social sciences than any other natural science. Such an approach does not contribute to satisfying the unique "historical interest" that is closely linked to the possibility of interpretive understanding. Constructs such as the "law of marginal utility" are actually valuable for the social sciences precisely because "they contain not a shred of 'psychology' in any possible sense of that term" (Weber, 1903–1906/1975, note p. 85). He reiterates this position in other methodological writings (see Weber, 1922, Chap. 1), emphasizing that the reference to the meaning of action for the actor, which is supported by the understanding sociology ("Verstehende Soziologie"), has nothing to do with the treatment of psychical processes by psychology.[10]

Consequently, according to Weber, it is the "consciously purposeful" actions that are of central interest to the social sciences. These actions can be explained by means of constructs involving teleological models of rational action that are heuristically fruitful "for the causal analysis of historical interconnections." In this perspective, these constructs can take on a purely individual character, representing interpretive hypotheses related to concrete individual contexts, or a general nature, in the form of ideal-typical constructs. These teleological models of rational action have partly a priori status. Their relationship to observable reality is correlational in nature (involving connections between two distinct universes that respectively belong to the theoretical and observational realms). Thus, Weber's emphasis on the idea of empirical or causal adequacy complements the notion of adequacy at the level of meaning, which derives from the social sciences' understanding the mode of action of their basic units from within. This is why Weber also argues that, in contrast to "empirical laws," whose causal interpretation is problematic, it is the empirical validity of "a teleological model of rational action" that is problematic (Weber, 1903–1906/1975, note p. 84).

Another difference with the natural sciences is that in the social sciences, knowledge of causal relations refers to the singular historical and cultural contexts from which the meaning of actions is defined, and not to conceptual generalizations that, by emphasizing common causal factors, tend to distance theoretical models from observable reality. The interpretive capacity of the social actor in general, and of the social science observer in particular, implies relating the actions of individuals to the specific contexts in which they occur by understanding those actions interpretively in relation to those contexts. If we want to understand the phenomena in question, we must refer to the singular causal relations that underlie them and that are "intelligible to our inner experience."

> The course of human action and every sort of human expression are susceptible to meaningful interpretation (…) The [understanding] interpretation opens the possibility of taking this step beyond what is 'given'; and, in spite of Rickert's objections, it is this possibility that provides the specific justification for classifying as a special group ([viz.] the sciences of the human spirit) those sciences which employ such interpretations for method[olog]ical purposes.
>
> (Weber, 1903–1906/1975, note pp. 10–11)

Weber goes on to explain:

> The goal of the analysis is not to find bacteriological laws (to take one example), but to provide a causal explanation of "facts" of cultural history. And because of the nature of the concept of "culture", this invariably means that [the historical analysis] will as its culmination lead to knowledge of a context which understandable human action (or, more generally, 'behavior') is conceived as being fitted into and influenced by – because that is what 'historical' interest is concerned with.
>
> (Weber, 1903–1906/1975, p. 54)

Weber thus underlines the idea of a connection between causes in the social sciences and the reasons of social actors, which he emphasizes in his methodological introduction to *Economy and Society*:

> Sociology (in the sense given here to this very ambiguous word) is a science that aims to understand social action interpretively [*deutend verstehen*] and thus to explain its course and effects causally.
>
> (Weber, 1922, § 1)

The causal role of the situations of social actors, which implies the Simmelian forms associated with the idea of culture evoked above, is thus largely indirect, mediated by how the social actors themselves interpret their situations. It is based on processes that do not belong to the natural sciences but are related to the semantic nature of the phenomena of consciousness and, in this respect, imply human rational capacity in the broadest sense (see Bulle 2022). This broad rational capacity justifies the very idea of understanding interpretation, which relies on the observer's ability to comprehend the subjective context of meaning underlying individual "actions". It thus discards assumptions about "irrational" influences that are not meaningful to social actors. Therefore, the understanding approach is diametrically opposed to the forms of causal explanation that imply a direct influence of collective entities on individual actions in historicism. We know that at the end of his life, Weber wrote to Robert Liefmann, a marginalist economist:

> If I have now become a sociologist (according to my documents of appointment!) [chair at the University of Munich in 1919] it is to a large measure because I want to put an end to the whole business - which still has not been laid to rest - of working with collective concepts [*Kollektivbegriffe*]. In other words, sociology, too, can only be pursued by taking as one's point of departure the actions[11] of one, or more (few or many) individuals, that is to say, with a strictly "individualistic" method. [*Soziologie muss auch in der Methode strikt individualistisch betrieben werden*].
>
> (Weber, Letter to Robert Liefmann dated March 9 1920)[12]

Finally, it is essential to acknowledge the intrinsic link between MI and the understanding approach and, in this respect, the intrinsic link between the individual and social levels of explanation through the problematic of meaning.

The term "methodological individualism" came into widespread use only a few decades after Weber's contribution, with Hayek's and Popper's attacks on historicism in the early 1940s. It can be found in a chapter subtitle of Mises' (1949) *Human Action*: "The Principle of Methodological Individualism," where Mises counters the charge that the individualist method entails reductionism:

> The controversy whether the whole or its parts are logically prior is vain. Logically the notions of a whole and its parts are correlative. As logical concepts they are both apart from time [...] It is uncontested that in the sphere of human action social entities have real existence. Nobody ventures to deny that nations, states, municipalities, parties, religious communities, are real factors determining the course of human events. Methodological individualism, far from contesting the significance of such collective wholes, considers it as one of its main tasks to describe and to analyze their becoming and their disappearing, their changing structures, and their operation. And it chooses the only method fitted to solve this problem satisfactorily. First, we must realize that all actions are performed by individuals. A collective operates always through the intermediary of one or several individuals whose actions are related to the collective as the secondary source. It is the meaning which the acting individuals and all those who are touched by their action attribute to an action, that determines its character. It is the meaning that marks one action as the action of an individual and another action as the action of the state or of the municipality. The hangman, not the state, executes a criminal. It is the meaning of those concerned that discerns in the hangman's action an action of the state.
>
> (Mises, 1949/1998, pp. 78–79)

1.8 Methodological individualism from past to present

This brief introduction touches only on some of the important milestones that have helped to lay the foundations of methodological individualism, which, as Weber pointed out, does not claim to encompass the entire field of social science. Nevertheless, MI deserves special recognition as a method with an explanatory purpose, even if the notions of explanation and description have only relative values.

The individualist method developed in struggles against the approaches in the social sciences inherited from classical empiricism, in which causal relations link discrete units, as well as against the functional forms of causality derived from the natural sciences, in explaining human behavior. On the one hand, the founders of MI defended the similarity of the explanatory ambitions of the social sciences and the natural sciences by implementing, in theoretical models, basic units whose diverse arrangements or interactions can account for observable changes. On the other hand, they claimed that the social sciences differ fundamentally from the natural sciences in their ability to understand internally the causal processes at work. According to the individualist method they advocated, social actors are the basic units of analysis. The principle of rationality involved reflects their general capacity to interpret their situation and, consequently, to ascribe meaning to their action, so that this meaning explains their reasons for acting, which formally represent the cause of their action. This rational capacity, which they share with the observer and which brings into play an interpretive dimension rooted in their social being, serves as the explanatory principle that intrinsically links MI to "understanding" sociology. Within this framework, the founders of MI defended the importance of referring to the subjective meaning of actions through abstract constructs, and of analyzing the effects, especially the unintended ones, of the composition of individual actions. In doing so, they fought against the naturalization of the human subject in the various forms of historicism that dominated the 19th century and fed the extremisms of the 20th century.

The reflections of the early proponents of MI show that its core truth is not reducible to the notion that only individuals have the power to act, an assumption commonly accepted by social scientists: The individualism in MI is basically methodological. In this respect, the essential distinction between MI and the various forms of (causal) holism (which attribute causal action to wholes separate from their parts) lies in the processes that underlie the action of individuals as members of society or particular social groups. This distinction concerns the factors considered in the explanation. MI excludes the recourse, explicit or implicit, to irrational factors, that is, to factors that cannot be imputed to the meaningful experiences, interpretive processes, and motives of the subjects themselves. In this way, MI contrasts with the direct causal effect that the observer tends to ascribe to abstract social constructs. These constructs, referring to collective entities, are assumed to explain the influence of social factors on individual actions through the same types of causes as in the natural sciences. Examples include the notion of the "people's spirit" or, in relation to more recent forms of holism, that of the "class habitus." The explanatory value of these constructs is misleading and involves what MI calls the misuse of collective concepts.[13] The causal impact of social situations on individual actions is seen as mostly indirect in MI, shaped by their influence on the individuals' reasons for acting. Moreover, the ability of the social actors to give meaning to these situations (principle of rationality) is inherent in their social nature. Consequently, MI stands in opposition to any reductionist approach that would imply that individuals have causal properties independent of their social nature.[14]

Among the contemporary exponents of MI, James Coleman (1990) is without doubt the most familiar to the Anglo-Saxon public, but he remains a heterodox representative of MI, favoring a pragmatic conception of explanation, as shown by his support for classical rational choice theory (RCT).[15] Following the path of the founders, with a tendency to identify methodological traces of MI in the most relevant analyses of sociology, regardless of their doctrinal origins, Raymond Boudon is one of the principal contemporary proponent of MI.[16] His 1973 book *Education, Opportunity, and Social Inequality* is a notable example of the successful application of MI to the phenomenon of social reproduction, challenging the then-dominant culturalist and neo-Marxist models. Another prominent proponent of MI is Jon Elster, who demonstrated the relevance of the individualist method in *Making Sense of Marx* (Elster, 1985). However, it would be impossible to list all those who, without explicitly claiming MI affiliation, use the individualist method as part of good social science research practice.

Despite the numerous works and achievements within the interpretive framework of MI, some researchers continue to fight it, but with strawman arguments. The fact that methodological battles continue is undoubtedly a good thing and a necessity in order to constantly stimulate thinking, clarify it, and adapt it to changing issues and knowledge. However, the repetition of unfounded criticisms without valid references to MI theory and practice should alert the scientific community to its modes of control and its true cognitive goals. Now, with a clear understanding of the foundations of MI, a wide range of interpretations becomes available, possibly accepting or rejecting some of the assumptions of its founders, or helping to refine, develop, and illuminate them.[17]

Notes

1 Cf Simmel (1907)'s foreword to the third edition.
2 The Lamarckian theory of the heredity of acquired characteristics was still endorsed by Spencer.
3 But Weber does not rule out the possibility that certain genetically inherited unconscious attitudes, if proven, might be considered data for the understanding approach, just as other data are.
4 Menger emphasizes that this is not in itself a dishonor, but implies adherence to a series of scientific convictions, among which the most important is that the free play of individual interests is most favorable to the economic common good.
5 Emile Meyerson's anthropology of knowledge (1908/1989), seems to be anticipated here by Menger. Meyerson explains that the principle of causality that we apply in scientific explanation is based on the belief in an internal order of nature. What reconciles observable change and postulated order is the assumption that certain fundamental properties of things persist over time and that only their arrangement changes, so that our understanding can be based on these persistent properties and the consideration that their possible arrangements underlie the various observable phenomena. This idea was already in the air in Menger's time, since Meyerson quotes Maxwell (on the natural sciences): "When a physical phenomenon can be completely described as a change in the configuration and motion of a material system, the dynamical explanation of that phenomenon is said to be complete. We

cannot conceive any further explanation to be either necessary, desirable, or possible, for as soon as we know what is meant by the words configuration, motion, mass, and force, we see that the ideas which they represent are so elementary that they cannot be explained by means of anything else" (Clerk-Maxwell, 1875, p. 357).

6　Mill formally defines "Ethology" (in one of his letters to Auguste Comte, dated October 30, 1843) as: "*la théorie de l'influence des diverses circonstances extérieures, soit individuelles, soit sociales, sur la formation du caractère moral et intellectuel* [the theory of the influence of various external circumstances, either individual or social, on the formation of moral and intellectual character]."

7　While studying law at the University of Vienna from 1901 to 1906, Schumpeter developed an interest in sociology and economics. However, the earliest evidence of their mutual acquaintance dates back to the early 1910s. It is known that Weber commissioned Schumpeter to write a handbook on economics entitled *Grundriss der Sozialökonomik* (Swedberg 1991), whose English translation in 1954 was *Economic Doctrine and Method: An Historical Sketch*.

8　The second edition, published in 1905, is a considerably enlarged version compared to the first edition from 1892, while the third edition, released in 1907, includes some addenda.

9　See especially Popper (1978).

10　Weber is referring here to psychological approaches that study the "psychic" with the means of the natural sciences. In contrast, understanding sociology uses a form of abstract psychology (as Simmel puts it), which involves a theoretical reconstruction in terms of conscious processes.

11　Let us recall that Weber specifies in *Economy and Society* that human behavior is called "action" "if and insofar as the acting individual or individuals attach a subjective meaning to it" (Weber, 1922, § 1).

12　See Braun and Whimster (2014, p. 410).

13　See, for example, Hayek (1943, p. 45): "Instead of reconstructing the wholes from the relations between individual minds which we directly know, a vaguely apprehended whole is treated as something akin to the individual mind. It is in this form that in the social sciences an illegitimate use of anthropomorphic concepts has had as noxious an effect as the use of such concepts in the natural sciences."

14　This point is developed in Bulle (2023).

15　Particularly adapted to mathematical modeling, classical RCT models posit that individuals are driven by consequentialist motivations, self-interest goals, and decision-making processes based on cost-benefit calculations.

16　For an introduction to his work, see, for instance, Leroux and Robitaille (2024, *forthcoming*).

17　For further reading on this subject, see especially the various contributions to *The Palgrave Handbook of Methodological Individualism* I edited with Francesco Di Iorio (2023).

References

Arendt, H. (1958). *The human condition.* Chicago: University of Chicago Press.

Bostaph, S. (1978). The methodological debate between Carl Menger and the German historicists. *Atlantic Economic Journal, 6*(3), 3–16.

Boudon, R. (1973/1974). *Education, opportunity, and social inequality; Changing prospects in western society.* New York: Wiley.

Boudon, R. (1984). Introduction. In Simmel, G. (1984 [1907]). *Les problèmes de la philosophie de l'histoire* [Problems of the philosophy of history] (pp. 7–52). Paris: PUF.

Boudon, R. (2008). Mais où sont les théories générales d'antan ? [But where are the general theories of yesterday?]. *European Journal of Social Sciences, 140*, 31–50.

Braun, H. H. and Whimster, S. (2014). Max Weber: Collected methodological writings. London: Routledge.

Bulle, N. (2022). Rationality as a meta-analytical capacity of the human mind: From the social sciences to Gödel. *Philosophy of the Social Sciences, 53*(3),167–193.

Bulle, N. (2023). Methodological individualism as holism of the parts. In N. Bulle & F. Di Irio (Eds.), *The Palgrave handbook of methodological individualism*. New York: Palgrave Macmillan.

Bulle, N., & Di Iorio, F. (Eds.). (2023). *The Palgrave handbook of methodological individualism*. New York: Palgrave Macmillan.

Clerk-Maxwell, J. (1875). On the dynamical evidence of the molecular constitution of bodies. *Nature, 11*(279), 357–359.

Coleman, J. S. (1990). *Foundations of social theory*. Cambridge: Harvard University Press.

Elster, J. (1985). *Making sense of Marx*. Cambridge: Cambridge University Press.

Hayek, F. (1942). Scientism and the study of society. Part I. *Economica, 9*(35), 267–291.

Hayek, F. (1943). Scientism and the study of society. Part II. *Economica, 10*(37), 34–63.

Hayek, F. (1944). Scientism and the study of society. Part III. *Economica, 11*(41), 27–39.

Hayek, F. (1955). *The counter-revolution of science*. New York: Free Press.

Hayek, F. (1980) Preface. In Schumpeter J. A. (1980 [1908]). *Methodological individualism* (p. 1). Brussels: Institutum Europaeum.

Leroux, R., & Robitaille, C. (2024). *Anthem companion to Raymond Boudon*. London: Anthem Press.

Mandelbaum, M. (1971). *History, man and reason, a study in nineteenth-century thought*. Baltimore: The John Hopkins Press.

Menger, C. (1883). *Untersuchungen uber die Methode der Socialwissenschaften und der Politischen Oekonomie insbesondere* [*Investigations into the method of the social sciences with special reference to economics*]. Leipzig: Verlag von Duncker & Humblot.

Menger, C. (1884/1935). *Collected works volume III*. London: London School of Economics.

Meyerson, E. (1908/1989). *Identity and reality*. London: Routledge.

Mill, J. S. (1843). The logic of the moral sciences. In *A system of logic, book 6*. London: John W. Parker.

Peukert, H. (2001). The Schmoller renaissance. *History of Political Economy, 33*(1), 71–116.

Popper, K. (1944a). The poverty of historicism, I. *Economica, 11*(42), 86–103.

Popper, K. (1944b). The poverty of historicism, II. A criticism of historicist methods. *Economica, 11*(43), 119–137.

Popper, K. (1945). The poverty of historicism, III. *Economica, 12*(46), 69–89.

Popper, K. (1957). The Poverty of Historicism. Boston: Beacon Press.

Popper, K. (1945/1966). *The open society and its enemies*. London: Routledge.

Popper, K. (1978, April 7). *Three worlds. The tanner lecture on human values.* Delivered at The University of Michigan.

Pribram, K. (1983). *A history of economic reasoning.* Baltimore: Johns Hopkins University Press.

Schmoller, G. (1900). *Grundriss der allgemeinen Volkswirtschaftslehre [Outlines of economic science].* Leipzig: Duncker & Humblot.

Schumpeter, J. A. (1908/2009). *The nature and essence of economic theory.* New Brunswick, New Jersey. Trans-Action [*Transaction. Das Wesen und der Hauptinhalt der theoretischen Nationalökonomie*]. Leipzig: Verlag von Duncker.

Simmel, G. (1907/1905). *From Die Probleme der Geschichtsphilosophie [The problems of the philosophy of history].* Leipzig: Duncker & Humblot.

Simmel, G. (1896/1897). How social forms maintain themselves. *The Sociological Year,* 71–109.

Swedberg, R. (1991). *Schumpeter his life and work.* Malden, MA: Polity Press.

Thilly, F. (1923). The individualism of John Stuart Mill. *The Philosophical Review, 32*(1), 1–17.

von Mises, L. (1949/1998). *Human action a treatise on economics.* Auburn, AL: Ludwig von Mises Institute.

Weber, M. (1903–1906/1975). *Roscher and Knies: The logical problems of historical economics.* London: Routledge.

Weber, M. (1922/1949). *The methodology of the social sciences* (E. A. Shils & H. A. Finch, Trans and Eds.). Glencoe: The Free Press.

Weber, M. (1922). *Wirtschaft und Gesellschaft [Economy and society].* Tübingen: Mohr Siebeck.

2 Carl Menger (1883)

On the theoretical understanding of social phenomena that are neither the products of convention nor of positive legislation, but the unintended results of historical development[1]

2.1 That the recognition of social phenomena as organic structures does not exclude the search for an exact (atomistic) understanding of them

> The theoretical understanding of natural organisms can also be twofold: exact (atomistic, physical-chemical) or empirical-realistic (collectivistic, specifically anatomical-physiological). - The exact understanding of natural organisms is not only sought in the natural sciences but represents an advance over the empirical-realistic understanding. - The exact understanding of social phenomena, or parts of them, cannot be dismissed on the grounds that the phenomena in question are perceived as "social organisms." - The fact that the exact understanding of natural organisms and their functions has so far only been partially achieved does not prove that this goal is unattainable with regard to the so-called social organisms. - The theory that "organisms" are indivisible wholes and that their functions represent vital expressions of these structures in their entirety does not oppose the exact (atomistic) orientation of theoretical research, whether in the field of natural or that of so-called social organisms. - The exact orientation of social research does not deny the real unity of social organisms; rather, it seeks to explain their nature and origin in an exact manner. Furthermore, it does not deny the validity of the empirical-realistic orientation of research in the field of the aforementioned phenomena.

In the previous chapter, we discussed the analogy between social phenomena and natural organisms, the limits of its validity, and finally the implications for social sciences methodology. It turned out that this analogy is only a partial one and that, even in those aspects where it is relevant, it is only a superficial one. Consequently, the understanding of those phenomena that do not point to a pragmatic origin but are the results of "organic," that is, unintended, processes, cannot be achieved by merely drawing an analogy with natural

DOI: 10.4324/9781032627021-2

organisms nor by transposing the perspectives of physiology and anatomy to social research.

We must now examine how those problems of social research, the solutions of which cannot be obtained through the "pragmatic" approach, given the objective state of affairs, and which have thus far been addressed "organically" on the basis of the aforementioned analogy, can be resolved in a manner that is both adequate for the nature of social phenomena and aligned with the specific goals of theoretical research in this field.

However, before delving into the problems that interest us, we would like to make some general remarks.

As we have seen above, all theoretical understanding of phenomena can result from a dual orientation of research: empirical-realistic and exact. This holds true not only in general but also for each specific area of phenomena. Even the understanding of those social phenomena that are based on an unintended or, if one prefers, an 'organic' process, or indeed, even the understanding of natural organisms themselves, can be achieved through the two above-mentioned orientations of research. Only the combination of the two can provide us with the deepest theoretical understanding of the phenomena in question that is attainable in our time.

This does not mean that both types of theoretical understanding have already been effectively achieved in the same way in all fields of phenomena, or, with regard to the present state of the theoretical sciences of the organic world, that they can even be regarded as attainable with certainty. As a postulate of research, the exact understanding of phenomena stands on an equal footing with the empirical-realistic understanding in all fields of phenomena, in that of "organic social formations" as well as in that of natural organisms. It is possible that the exact analysis of natural organisms will never succeed completely and that empirical-realistic research will always remain indispensable for their theoretical understanding, at least in some respects. It is possible that the physical-chemical (atomistic!) understanding of them will never achieve exclusive dominance, if only for the aforementioned reason. The empirical-realistic conception of the organic world is a justified one at the present, perhaps one that can continue to be justified alongside the atomistic conception.

Only someone unfamiliar with the current state of theoretical research in the field of natural organisms could conclude that the aspiration for an exact (atomistic) understanding of natural organisms is generally unjustified or even unscientific. "Physiology," says Helmholtz, "has had to decide to come to terms with the unconditional compliance of natural forces to laws even in the study of life processes; it has had to take seriously the fact that they follow physical and chemical processes taking place within organisms." Another distinguished researcher believes that the physical-chemical understanding of organic phenomena constitutes precisely a criterion for the development of the theoretical sciences of the organic world.

It has been said that the exact analysis of natural organisms has been only partially successful, and perhaps it will never be completely successful; but it would be to ignore the progress of the exact natural sciences to overlook the extent of what has already been achieved in this respect – the successes of "atomism" in the field of natural organisms – or to characterize the above-mentioned efforts toward an exact understanding of the organic world as an unscientific aberration.

Consequently, even those who adhere to the theory of the strict analogy between social phenomena and natural organisms cannot reject the atomistic orientation of research in the social sciences. On the contrary, those who constantly refer to this analogy should also consistently support the aspirations of natural scientists to achieve an exact (atomistic!) understanding of the organic world and be far removed from a one-sided appreciation of the empirical-realistic approach to research. The problem we intend to address in this chapter can thus be designated as the problem of the 'organic' world. This is without prejudice to the fact that, in addition to the empirical-realistic understanding of the social formations and their functions, their exact understanding is a legitimate goal of theoretical research. Recognizing a set of social phenomena as "organisms" is in no way inconsistent with striving for an exact (atomistic!) understanding of them.

But what about the approach of those who, because exact understanding has so far been achieved only imperfectly in the realm of natural organisms, conclude that the pursuit of such understanding in the realm of social phenomena, which can only truly be called organisms in a metaphorical sense, is unjustified and even unscientific? On the contrary, is it not clear that even if an exact understanding of natural organisms were quite unattainable and even inappropriate for this realm of the phenomenal world, this same understanding would not necessarily be excluded from the realm of social phenomena? Is it not obvious that the question of whether such an understanding would be possible can always and only be answered by an original study that takes the nature of social phenomena directly into account and never by a superficial analogy?[2]

If the belief that, in the realm of social phenomena, only the "organic" or, more precisely, the "collectivist" conception is justified, or even "superior" to the exact conception, has nevertheless found so many proponents in recent sociological literature, it is because of a misunderstanding which, due to its fundamental importance, should be briefly addressed here.

A widespread objection to the exact solution of theoretical problems in the field of social phenomena arises from the fact that social formations, like natural organisms, are indivisible wholes, higher units in relation to their parts, that their functions are vital manifestations of the organic structures as a whole, and that the striving for an exact interpretation of their essence and functions, the "atomistic" point of view in the theories of the organic world, therefore means a misjudgment of this unitary essence.

We have already pointed out that this view is by no means shared by the natural sciences, since the exact interpretation of organic phenomena is one of the highest goals of modern research in this field. We also aim to demonstrate that this viewpoint is untenable in the area of social research and that it is, in fact, based on a fundamental misconception.

The sciences, as a whole, are supposed to provide us with an understanding of all aspects of reality, with the theoretical sciences specifically providing a theoretical understanding of the real world. This is true even for those theoretical sciences devoted to the study of organisms. But they could only achieve this goal imperfectly if they neglected the true unity of the phenomena in question. If they present the phenomena only as a collection of parts rather than a whole, and if the functions of organisms are not depicted in their entirety, then their purpose would be inadequately fulfilled.

However, the fact that organisms always present themselves to us as a whole and their functions as vital expressions of them in their totality does not imply that the exact orientation of research is generally unsuitable for them, or that only an empirical-realistic orientation of theoretical research is appropriate for this group of phenomena. What this circumstance does imply for theoretical research in the realm of organisms is that it poses a number of challenges for exact research, which cannot be ignored by the latter. These challenges concern the exact interpretation of the nature and origin of organisms (considered as units) and the exact interpretation of their functions.

Therefore, the exact orientation of research in the realm of the organic world does not deny the unity of organisms; on the contrary, it aims to explain the origin and functions of these unitary structures in an exact way, and it seeks to elucidate how these "real units" came into being and how they operate.

This task, which ranks among the highest in modern natural science, is also undertaken by the exact orientation of research in the realm of social phenomena, especially those that appear as unintended products of historical development. Consequently, it is not a matter of ignoring the "unity" of social organisms, as long as it corresponds to real situations. Rather, the aim of the research is, on the one hand, to elucidate the particular nature of the "unity" of those formations conceived as social organisms and, on the other hand, to offer an exact explanation of their origin and function. It does not indulge in the illusion that this unity can be understood merely by analogy with natural organisms but seeks, through direct investigation, through observation of the "social organisms" themselves, to deepen their unitary essence. It is not content with attempting to understand the functions of the social formations in question through the above analogy but aspires to their exact understanding. Far from considering analogies, it demonstrates their inadequacy. It seeks to achieve for the social sciences, through direct investigation of the social formations, the very goal that the exact orientation of theoretical research in the field of natural organisms seeks to achieve, namely the exact understanding of the so-called "social organisms" and their functions. It opposes an understanding of social formations based on mere analogies for general methodological reasons, for the very reasons that, for example, would justify the opposition of physiology to a "politico-economical" understanding of the human organism as a research principle; it rejects the view that theoretical problems that have not yet been solved in the field of the study of nature or that appear insolvable in our time should also be considered unsolvable in the field of social research. On the contrary, it studies these problems without regard to the results of physiology and anatomy, limiting itself to the social formations themselves, just as physiology, in its search for an empirical or exact understanding of natural organisms, does not concern itself with the results of social research; all this, however, without disregarding the unitary nature of social organisms, but for general methodological reasons.[3]

The opinion that the unitary nature of these social formations, called "social organisms," excludes the exact interpretation (the atomistic interpretation!) of them is therefore a gross misunderstanding. In the following, however, we will first deal with the exact understanding of "social organisms" and their functions, and then proceed to their empirical-realistic understanding.

2.2 On the various orientations of theoretical research that result from viewing social phenomena as "organic" structures

> A portion of the social formations is of pragmatic origin and must therefore be interpreted pragmatically. - Another portion of them is the unintended result of social development (of "organic" origin!), and their pragmatic interpretation cannot be admitted. - The main challenge to the theoretical interpretation of the origin of the social formations that developed unintentionally (in an "organic" way). - The above-mentioned challenge and the main problems of theoretical economics are closely related. – Two other issues of theoretical social science in general and of theoretical economics in particular that result from the "organic" conception of social phenomena: a) the aspiration to understand the interdependence of social phenomena; b) the aspiration to understand social phenomena as functions and vital manifestations of society (or national economy, etc.) conceived as an organic whole. - The pursuit of exact (atomistic!) and empirical-realistic (collectivist, anatomical-physiological!) solutions to the above problems.

There is a whole series of social phenomena which are the product of the agreement of the members of society or of positive legislation and which thus result from the purposeful community activity of society, conceived as a separate acting entity. These are social phenomena for which there can be no question of an "organic" origin in any admissible sense. In these cases, the pragmatic interpretation – explaining the nature and origin of the aforementioned social phenomena on the basis of the intentions, opinions, and available resources of social groups or their leaders – is the approach that corresponds to the actual situation.

We interpret these phenomena pragmatically by examining the aims that led the social groups or their leaders to create and develop the social phenomena in question in each specific case, the means that were available to them for this purpose, the obstacles that stood in the way of the creation and development of these social formations, and the way in which the available means were used to create them. This task is all the more perfect the more we study the ultimate real goals of the individuals who acted, on the one hand, and the initial means at their disposal, on the other, and the more we have learned to understand the social phenomena that point to a pragmatic origin as links in a chain of decisions aimed at achieving the aforementioned ends. We make a historical-pragmatic critique of social phenomena of this kind, examining in each case the real goals of social groups or their leaders in relation to the needs of the social groups concerned and the use of the means of social action in relation to the conditions of success (the fullest possible satisfaction of social needs).

All of this applies to social phenomena that trace back to a pragmatic origin. As mentioned earlier, another part of them does not result from the agreement of the members of society or from legislation. Language, religion, law, even the state itself, and, to mention more specifically some social phenomena of an economic nature, the phenomena of markets, competition, money, and many other social formations already appear to us in historical epochs when there can be no question of their having been founded voluntarily by a deliberate activity of the communities as such or their leaders. We are dealing here with the emergence of social institutions that largely serve the welfare of society, often even vitally so, and yet are not the result of the social activity of the community. Here is the curious, perhaps the most curious, problem of the social sciences: *How is it that institutions which serve the common good and are of great importance for its development can come into being without a **common will** to create them?*

The problem of the theoretical interpretation of those social phenomena that do not trace back to a pragmatic origin in the above sense is not yet exhausted. There exist a number of highly significant social phenomena that have an "organic" origin, precisely in the same sense as the social formations described above. However, because they do not appear in their respective concrete forms as social "institutions" such as law, money, markets, etc., they are generally not conceived as "organic formations" and are therefore not interpreted in this way.

We could list a long series of phenomena of this kind, but we intend to illustrate our point with an example whose obviousness leaves no doubt as to the meaning of what we propose to explain here: We refer to the price of goods in society. As is well known, in some cases, prices are wholly or partly the result of deliberate social factors – such as taxes, wage laws, and so forth – but in general, they form and fluctuate without direct state intervention or explicit social agreements. Instead, they emerge as unintended consequences of social change. The same is true of interest on capital, land rents, corporate profits, and so on.

What is the nature of all the social phenomena mentioned above? This is the crucial question for our science – and how can we achieve a complete understanding of their nature and development?

It is hardly necessary to point out that the problem of the origin of social formations that have developed unintentionally and that of the emergence of those economic phenomena to which we have just referred exhibit a strong similarity. Law, language, the state, money, markets – all these social formations in their various manifestations and in their constant evolution are, to a large extent, the unintended results of social change. Prices of goods, interest rates, land rents, wages, and thousands of other phenomena of social life in general and of the economy in particular share the same characteristics, namely, that their understanding, in the cases discussed here, cannot be "pragmatic," but must be analogous to that of social institutions that have developed unintentionally. The solution to the main problems of theoretical social science in general and of theoretical economics in particular is closely related to the question of the theoretical understanding of the origin and change of social formations that have developed in an "organic" manner.

Here we must mention two other problems of theoretical social science, which are also rooted in the organic conception of social phenomena.

It has already been emphasized above, where reference was made to the analogy between natural organisms and various formations of social life in general and of economic life in particular, that the observer of the latter is confronted with a collection of institutions, each of which serves the normal function of the whole, conditions and influences it, and which, in turn, is conditioned and influenced by this whole in its normal essence and function. In a series of social phenomena, we also see this mutual conditioning between the normal functions of the whole and the normal functions of the parts, with, as a natural consequence, a particular orientation of research in the social sciences aimed at revealing this mutual conditioning of social phenomena.

In addition to this orientation of theoretical social research, another closely related approach could be called "organic" for the same reasons, namely, the one that attempts to make us understand economic phenomena as functions and vital manifestations of the whole national economy (conceived as an organic unity!). It thus holds a relationship, which we shall not discuss in detail, with certain problems of theoretical research in the realm of natural organisms.

All these orientations of research resulting from the organic conception of society (or of the economy), and the corresponding epistemological and theoretical principles, can rightly attract the attention of social philosophers.

However, the empirical-realistic (especially physiological) orientations of social science research have recently been developed so comprehensively, especially in Germany, that we can dispense with presenting them in detail and limit ourselves to the exact interpretation of the so-called organic social structures. In the following, therefore, we will deal with the aspiration to an exact understanding of those social formations which have been formed in unintentional ways, both those which are generally held to be "organisms" and those whose "organic" character has not been sufficiently emphasized so far. However, we will precede these explanations with an outline of the main attempts which have been made so far to solve the problems resulting from the organic conception of social phenomena.

2.3 On the attempts made so far to solve the problems resulting from the organic conception of social phenomena

> Pragmatism as a universal mode of explaining the origin and change of social phenomena. - Its contradiction with the teachings of history. - Interpreting the origin of the social formations that developed unintentionally by characterizing them as "organic", as "primitive." - Aristotle's opinion. - The aspiration to an organic understanding of the development of the social phenomena. - Their conception as functions and manifestations of the life of real social organisms (society, political economy, etc.) in their totality. - The aspiration to understand the reciprocal conditioning of social phenomena. - The physiological-anatomical orientation of social science research.

The first idea that came to understand social institutions, their nature, and their development was to explain them as the result of human calculations aimed at their creation and design, to attribute them to agreements between people, that is, acts of positive legislation. This (pragmatic) mode of explanation was unsuited to real conditions and quite unhistorical; however, it offered the advantage of interpreting all social institutions, both those that appear to be the result of the common will of socially organized individuals and those for which such an origin is not demonstrable, from a unified and easily understandable perspective, an advantage that will never be underestimated by anyone who is familiar with scientific works and knows the history of their development.

The contradiction between the historical facts and the aforementioned mode of explanation (i.e., the exclusively pragmatic explanation of the origin and change of social phenomena), which is only formally satisfactory, had the effect that in scientific investigations into the problem addressed here, alongside the above, evidently one-sided mode of interpretation - some even in direct opposition to it - a series of attempts have been made, most of which are meaningless but document quite well the insufficiency of the "organic" conceptions of social phenomena.

It is to this category that belong all the attempts of those who believe they have already solved the above problem by identifying the process of formation in question as "organic." We may well call "organic" the process by which social formations develop without an act of common will. However, let us not assume that this image, or any mystical allusion attached to it, solves in the least the intriguing problem of social science to which we have referred above.

Another, equally unsatisfactory, attempt to address the problem at hand is a widespread theory that recognizes social institutions as something original, that is, already given with the very existence of human beings, not something that has evolved, but a primordial product of community life. This theory (which, incidentally, is transposed to social institutions created by positive laws through a peculiar mysticism by some of its adherents, who believe that a unitary principle is superior to historical truth and the logic of things) avoids the error of those who attribute all institutions to acts of positive common will. However, it clearly does not offer a solution to the problem at hand but only evades it. The origin of a phenomenon is by no means explained by asserting that it has been present since the beginning of time or that it arose primordially. Even leaving aside the question of the historical foundations of the theory, the first assertion implies an absurdity for any complex phenomenon, since such a phenomenon must have evolved at some point from its simpler elements. A social phenomenon, in particular, must have developed from individual factors, at least in its original form.[4] The second assertion, on the other hand, draws an analogy between the emergence of social institutions and that of natural organisms that is of no value in resolving the problem. It states that the former are not voluntary creations of the human mind, but it does not explain how they came to be. These attempts at interpretation are comparable to the approach of a naturalist who would like to solve the problem of the origin of natural organisms by referring to their "original" character, their "natural growth," or their "primordial development."

Theories that aim to solve the problem of the origin of unintended social formations "organically" are no more acceptable than the theories mentioned above, which interpret changes in social phenomena as "organic processes." It is hardly necessary to emphasize that the changes in social phenomena, to the extent that they are not the intended result of agreement among members of society or positive legislation, but an unintended product of social development, cannot be interpreted in a socio-pragmatic manner. It is equally obvious, however, that no understanding of the nature and laws governing the development of social phenomena can be achieved by merely referring to the "organic" or "primordial" character of the processes under discussion or by simple analogies between them and the changes observed in natural organisms. The worthlessness of this line of research is so obvious that there is nothing to add to what has already been said on the subject.

To truly address this significant challenge to social knowledge, we cannot rely on the superficial and, as we have seen, largely untenable analogies. The solution lies in examining social phenomena not through an "organic," "anatomical," or "physiological" lens, but in a distinctly sociological and scientific manner. Achieving this requires theoretical social research, the nature and primary orientations of which we have already indicated (the exact and the empirical-realistic).

We would like to mention here another orientation of social research, which also belongs to the "organic" approach to social phenomena. By this, we mean the effort to understand their mutual conditioning. This research orientation is based on the idea of the "reciprocal causality" of social phenomena, an idea whose value for a deep theoretical understanding of these phenomena, as we have already indicated elsewhere, is not entirely unquestionable. Nevertheless, this view is so close to the common understanding that it rightly deserves the attention of social scientists, at least as long as the exact understanding of the most complicated social phenomena has not been achieved.

It would be a mistake to consider this approach as the only justified one or even, as some would like, as "the method" of the social sciences, but it would be just as wrong to want to ignore its significance and usefulness for the theoretical understanding of social phenomena in general. The name given to this research orientation is a matter of terminology and has no objective importance from a methodological point of view; nevertheless, we still believe that it bears a certain resemblance, albeit not entirely clear, to certain orientations of theoretical research in the social sciences. The fact remains that the expressions we are discussing here are purely figurative, and they truly designate a specifically social orientation of theoretical research, which would be objectively justified even if there were no science of natural organisms in general, nor anatomy and physiology in particular. Whether one calls it "organic" or "physiological-anatomical," it is in fact a branch of the empirical-realistic orientation of theoretical social research.

2.4 On the exact (atomistic) "understanding" of the origin of social formations that are the unintended "result" of social development

> Introduction. Course of the presentation. - a) The origin of money: the appearance of money. - Its specificity. - The theory that money originated through an agreement or a law. - Plato, Aristotle, the jurist

Paulus. - Inadequacy of this theory. - Exact explanation of the origin of money. - b) The origin of a series of other social institutions: the emergence of localities, of states. - The emergence of the division of labor, of markets. – The influence of legislation. - Exact explanation of the origin of the aforementioned social formations. - c) Final remarks: general nature of the social-pragmatic origin and the so-called "organic" origin of social phenomena; their opposition. - The methods for the exact understanding of the origin of "organic" social formations and those for the solution of the main problems of exact economics are the same.

Introduction.

In the previous section, I outlined the attempts made so far to solve the aforementioned problem and pointed out their inadequacy. If there is to be a serious solution to this problem, it must be sought in ways other than those used so far.

However, I will first illustrate the theory of the origin of the social formations discussed here with some examples, such as the emergence of money, states, markets, etc., thus the emergence of social institutions that largely serve the interests of society and whose primary origin, in the majority of cases, cannot be attributed in any way to positive laws or other expressions of purposeful common will.

2.4.1   On the origin of money[5]

A phenomenon that has always posed considerable challenges to social philosophers is the fact that in the markets of almost all societies with economic cultures that have evolved to barter, certain goods have been readily accepted by everyone in exchange for the goods brought to the market. Initially, depending on the circumstances, these goods were cattle heads, animal skins, cowrie shells, cocoa beans, tea bricks, and so on. As the culture progressed, they expanded to include unmonetized metals and eventually coined metals. In fact, these goods were accepted even by people who had no immediate need for them or who had already satisfied that need sufficiently. In short, in barter markets, certain goods emerged from the whole and became mediums of exchange, or "money" in the broadest sense of the word. The fact that, in a market, one good is willingly given up by its owner in exchange for another that seems more useful is a phenomenon that resonates with common understanding. However, the idea that anyone offering goods for sale should be willing to exchange them for some other specific good, such as cattle, cocoa beans, or quantities of copper or silver (depending on the circumstances), even if they have no immediate need for these goods or have already fully satisfied their possible needs for them, while refusing other goods on the same basis, is a procedure that runs counter to the idea of individuals simply pursuing their own interests. It is therefore not surprising that even an exceptional thinker like Savigny found this puzzling and that it seemed impossible to explain this procedure in terms of individual human interests.[6]

The challenge for science here is to explain such a social phenomenon, where a similar mode of action exists among community members, and a collective interest is evident, but individual motives are elusive. In such a context, the idea of attributing the phenomenon to an agreement or legislative act readily comes to the fore, especially when considering the later form of money. Plato contended that money was "an agreed-upon token for barter,"[7] while Aristotle said that money came into being by agreement, not by nature but by law.[8] The jurist Paulus,[9] with a few exceptions, the medieval theorists of money, up to the national economists of our time,[10] shared this view.

Rejecting this view as wrong in principle would be a mistake, for history does indeed provide us with examples where certain goods have been declared money by law. However, it must be kept in mind that in most of these cases, the legal provision was clearly not intended to introduce a certain commodity as money but rather to acknowledge a commodity that had already become money. Nevertheless, it is certain that the institution of money, like other social institutions, can be introduced through convention or legislation, especially in the formation of new communities from elements of old culture, such as in the colonies. Moreover, it is beyond doubt that the development of the said institution in periods of more advanced economic culture generally occurs in the latter way. Therefore, the above opinion is partially justified.

The understanding of the social institution in question here is different, since it cannot be understood historically as the result of legislative action, since money emerged from the economic conditions of a people without such activity, that is, "primordially" or, as others express it, "organically." In this case, the above-mentioned pragmatic explanation is inadmissible, and the task of science is to help us understand the institution of money by explaining the process by which, in the course of the development of economic culture, without any explicit agreement between people or legislative acts, a certain commodity or set of commodities stands out from the rest and becomes money, that is, a commodity that everyone accepts in exchange for the goods they offer, even if they do not need it.

The explanation of the above phenomenon is based on the following considerations: As long as simple barter prevails among a people, economic actors pursue a single goal. In their exchange transactions, they exchange their surplus for only those goods for which they have an immediate need, rejecting those that they do not need at all or that are already in sufficient supply. In order to exchange the goods they desire, individuals who bring their surplus to the market must find not only someone who needs their goods but also someone who offers the goods they seek. It is this circumstance which, under the rule of pure barter, creates considerable obstacles to trade and restricts it within the narrowest limits.

A very effective solution to this problem, which had a significant impact on the circulation of goods, was found in the situation itself. Individuals could easily observe that certain goods, especially those that satisfied a widespread need, were more in demand on the market than others. Therefore, they were more likely to find among the potential buyers of these goods those who offered certain goods that they desired than if they went to the market with goods that were less easy to dispose of. For example, among a nomadic people, everyone knows from experience that if they bring cattle to the market, they will more easily find those who offer the goods they desire among the many who are willing to exchange for cattle than if they offer other goods with a limited number of buyers. This led individuals with less marketable goods to not only exchange them for the items they needed immediately, but also, if those items were unavailable, to exchange them for other goods they did not need immediately but were easier to sell. This approach may not directly achieve the ultimate goal of the economic operation (acquiring the desired goods!), but it gets them much closer to it.

The economic interests of the various individuals, therefore, as their individual interests become better known, lead them, without any agreement, without any legal constraint, and even without considering the general interest, to exchange their goods for others that are more easily sold, even if they do not satisfy their immediate needs. Naturally, this interest encourages them to continue exchanging goods that lend themselves particularly well to barter in the most convenient and economical way. Thus, under the powerful influence of custom, we witness the ubiquitous phenomenon that accompanies the development of economic culture: A certain number of goods that are the most saleable, transportable, durable, and easily divisible according to time and place become universally accepted in barter and thus can be exchanged for any other commodity. These goods are what our ancestors called Geld [money], from the word "gelten," which means "to be worth," "to make," or "to pay."

The great importance of custom in the origin of money is evident from an examination of the process just outlined by which certain goods become money. It is in the economic interest of every individual to exchange less saleable goods for more saleable, more durable, more divisible goods, etc., but such exchanges can only take place if the economic actors recognize this interest and are willing to accept, for the sake of exchangeability, a good that may be completely useless to them in itself. This understanding will never be acquired by all members of a society at the same time. Rather, it is always initially a certain number of economic actors who recognize the advantage of accepting more easily sellable goods in exchange for their own when the immediate exchange of their goods for the ones they need is impossible or highly uncertain. This advantage is in itself independent of the general recognition of a commodity as money, since such an exchange always and under all circumstances brings the economic actors considerably closer to their ultimate goal, which is the acquisition of the consumer goods they need.

As we know, there is no better way to enlighten people about their economic interests than by observing the economic successes of those who implement the appropriate means to achieve them. It is evident that nothing could have promoted the emergence of money as effectively as the most discerning and capable economic actors receiving highly marketable commodities against all others for their own economic advantage and over an extended period of time. Therefore, usage and custom have undoubtedly played a role in making the most marketable commodities those that were accepted in exchange for their goods, not only by many economic actors but ultimately by all.

Consequently, money, an institution of general interest in the noblest sense of the term, can, as we have seen, come into being through legislation, like other social institutions. But this is not its only mode of formation, nor even its most primitive. The latter is to be found in the process outlined above, the nature of which would be inadequately explained if it were simply described as "organic," or if money were identified with something "primitive," "original," and so on. On the contrary, the origin of money can only be truly understood if we accept that the social institution in question is the unreflected, unintended result of the specific individual aspirations of the members of a society.

2.4.2 The origin of a number of other social institutions in general and economic institutions in particular

In the same way, one can question the origin of a series of other social formations that serve the common good, or even condition it, without being the result of a social intention to promote it.

Even today, the creation of new settlements is rarely the result of a group of people with different dispositions and professions coming together with the intention of founding them and carrying them out in a planned way. Of course, such a way of creating new settlements is not excluded and is even proven by experience. As a rule, however, new settlements come into being "unintentionally," that is, through the mere pursuit of individual interests, which inadvertently, and without any real intention, lead to the aforementioned success in promoting the common interest. The first peasants who take possession of a territory, the first artisan who settles among them, generally have only their individual interests in mind, as do the first innkeeper, the first grocer, the first teacher, and so on. As the needs of the members of the society increase, other economic actors find it advantageous to engage in new occupations within the growing community, or to practice the existing ones more fully. In this way, an economic organization is gradually formed which best serves the interests of the members of the community, and without which the normal existence of the community would be inconceivable, even though this organization is not the result of the implementation of a common will to establish it. The latter generally appears only at an advanced stage of community development, and it does not bring about the establishment, but usually only the refinement of social formations that have developed organically.

The same is true of the origin of the state. No impartial person can doubt that an agreement among a number of people with a territory at their disposal can, under favorable conditions, lay the foundations of a community capable of development. Nor can it be reasonably doubted that, under the natural conditions of family power, new states capable of development may be founded by individual leaders or groups of such leaders, even without the consent of all the members of the new state. Therefore, the theory that this social structure, which we call a state, arises "organically" is one-sided in any case. But it is equally erroneous, and even more anti-historical, to theorize that all states originally came into being through agreements to establish them or through the conscious activity of individual leaders or groups of leaders directed to that end. There can be little doubt that, at least in the earliest periods of human development, states developed in the following way: Heads of families living side by side, not bound by any political ties, but only by the fact that they gradually recognized their individual interests and endeavored to pursue them (through the voluntary submission of the weaker to the protection of the stronger, the effective help that neighbors gave to neighbors in cases where one was subjected to violence and in circumstances where the welfare of the other inhabitants of a territory was also threatened, etc.). Without any special agreement, they arrived at a community and state organization, even if it was not yet fully developed. In some cases, conscious agreements to strengthen the community as such and various power relations may have facilitated the process of state formation. In other cases, however, the accurate recognition and pursuit of individual interests by heads of families living side by side with each other certainly led to the formation of states without such influences, or even without any consideration of the common interest on the part of individuals. Thus, even that social structure we call the state, at least in its most primitive forms, has been the unintended result of aspirations to serve individual interests.

In the same way, it could be shown that other social institutions, such as language, law, morality, and, above all, numerous economic institutions, have arisen without any explicit agreement, without any legislative constraint, and even without any consideration of the general interest, but only under the impulse of individual interests and as the result of the exercise of the latter. The organization of the circulation of goods in periodic markets held in certain places, the organization of society through the separation of occupations and the division of labor, the customs of trade, etc., all institutions which serve the most important purposes of the state and which serve in the most eminent manner the interests of the common good, and whose origin seems at first sight to point necessarily to convention or to the power of the state, are not originally the result of agreement, contract, law, or of a special consideration of individuals for the general interest, but the result of aspirations in the service of individual interests.

It is clear that legislative power often intervenes in this "organic" process, thus accelerating or modifying its results. As far as the very first beginnings of the formation of society are concerned, the unintentional emergence of social phenomena may in fact be the decisive factor. In the course of social development, the deliberate intervention of public authorities in social relations becomes more and more evident; institutions that are born "organically" are joined by those that are the result of purposeful social action. Institutions born organically find their refinement and further development through this deliberate action of public authorities oriented towards social aims. Today's monetary and market systems, today's law, the modern state, etc., offer many examples of institutions that appear to us as the result of the combined action of teleological individual and social forces, or, in other words, of "organic" and "positive" factors.

2.4.3 Final remarks

If we now examine the general nature of the process responsible for those social phenomena that are not the results of purposeful social factors but are the unintended consequences of social change, a process that can at least be called "organic" in contrast to the creation of social phenomena by deliberate legislation, the answer to the above question seems quite clear.

The characteristic element in the socially teleological emergence of social phenomena lies in the intention of society as such to create them, under the condition that they are the deliberate results of the collective will of society, perceived as an active entity, or of its leaders. On the other hand, social phenomena of "organic" origin are characterized by the fact that they are the unintended consequences of individual aspirations – that is, the individual interests of the members of society – and are therefore, in contrast to the social formations mentioned above, the unintended social results of individual purposeful factors.

Nevertheless, we believe that the above discussion has not only allowed us to reveal the true nature of the process to which a significant portion of social phenomena owe their origin, previously obscured by vague analogies or meaningless terms, but has also allowed us to achieve another significant result for the methodology of the social sciences.

We have already noted that a long series of economic phenomena that are not typically considered to be "organically" created "social formations," such as market prices, wages, interest rates, and so on, arose in much the same way as the social institutions discussed in the previous section. They, too, are generally not the results of purposeful social causes but the unintended consequences of the myriad efforts of economic actors to pursue individual interests. The theoretical understanding of the nature and development of these phenomena can therefore only be achieved in the same way as for the aforementioned social formations, namely by tracing back to their elements, that is, to the individual factors that caused them, and by studying the laws according to which the complex phenomena of human economy in question develop from these elements. It is hardly necessary to point out that this is the method we have previously described as the most suitable for guiding theoretical research in the field of social phenomena in general. Consequently, the method for accurately understanding the origins of "organically" created social formations and the method for addressing the main issues of exact economics are fundamentally identical.

Notes

1 Carl Menger (1883) *Untersuchungen über die Methode der Socialwissenschaften und der Politischen Oekonomie insbesondere* [*Investigations into the Method of the Social Sciences with Special Reference to Economics*] (Book 3 chap. 2, pp. 139–159).

2 The ultimate elements upon which the exact theoretical interpretation of natural phenomena must rest are "atoms" and "forces." Both are of a non-empirical nature. We cannot represent the "atoms" at all, nor the forces of nature, other than by an image, and in reality, we only understand them as causes of real movements that are unknown to us. This results in quite extraordinary difficulties for the exact interpretation of natural phenomena. The situation is different in the exact social sciences. Here, the ultimate elements of our analysis are human individuals and their aspirations, which are of empirical nature, giving the exact theoretical social sciences a significant advantage over the exact natural sciences. The "limits of the knowledge of nature" and the resulting difficulties for the theoretical understanding of natural phenomena do not really exist for the exact research in the realm of social sciences. When A[uguste] Comte conceives of "societies" as real organisms, even as organisms of a more complex nature than natural organisms, and when he designates their theoretical interpretation as an incomparably more complicated and challenging scientific problem, he commits a serious error. His theory would only be acknowledged by social scientists, who, given the current state of the theoretical natural sciences, would have the quite foolish idea of wanting to interpret the phenomena of society not in a specifically social-scientific way but rather in the atomistic-scientific way proper to the natural sciences.

3 The "organic," or more precisely, "collectivist," conception of economy is not opposed to the goals of theoretical political economy in general, nor does it encompass the entirety of the latter's tasks. It is merely a part, a specific aspect, of the science that teaches us to understand economic phenomena theoretically, and acknowledging it does not detract from the concept of economics as a theoretical science, nor does it alter it in any way. Also, the acknowledgment of the "organic" conception of political economy does not transform our science into a historical or practical science, nor into a science solely focused on the "organic" understanding of human economy (in the form of a simplistic "anatomo-physiology").

4   Obviously, such nonsense was alien to Aristotle as well, no matter how often he is
     cited as the founder of the theory that the state is something "original," given with
     the existence of humanity itself. See Appendix VII: "On the Opinion Ascribed to
     Aristotle that the State Is an Original Phenomenon Given Simultaneously with the
     Existence of Man."
5   See my *Grundsätze der Volkswirtschaftslehre* [*Principles of Economics*] (Menger,
     1871), pp. 250ff. where the above theory is already presented.
6   Savigny (1841), II, 406.
7   Plato, De Republica II, 12.
8   Aristotle, Ethic. Nicom. V, 8.
9   Corpus Juris Civilis: Digesta, Lib. 1, 18, 1.
10 Cf. the related literature in my *Volkswirthschaftslehre* [*Principles of Economics*]
     (Menger, 1871), pp. 255ff.

References

Aristotle. *Nicomachean ethics.*

Corpus juris civilis: Digesta.

Menger, C. (1871). *Grundsätze der Volkswirtschaftslehre [Principles of economics].*
    Wien: Wilhelm Braumüller.

Plato. *De republica.*

von Savigny, F. C. (1841). *System des heutigen Römischen Rechts [System of the
    present Roman law]* (Vol. II). Berlin: Veit & Comp.

3 Joseph Schumpeter (1908)

Methodological individualism and the emergence of the marginalist school of economics[1]

3.1 By way of introduction

Here is a brief overview of the most important approaches at this time. In doing so, we are following an old practice. Almost every economic work, especially the systematic ones, is preceded by such an overview. This has the advantage of informing the readers of the author's basic position and introducing them to the literature. We have to do this even though understanding our remarks already presupposes knowledge of the subject. We have another reason for doing so: We see it as our duty to contribute to a deeper understanding of each approach, to better delineate them, and, if possible, to establish a more precise relationship between them. To this end, some of the more important ones will be mentioned here, although at this stage we wish to discuss them impartially and dispassionately, and to be critical on only a few points. We are far from making sweeping judgments at the threshold of our explanations, as is often the case. Rather, a yardstick for criticism should only emerge for the reader from the totality of our discussions. In this general overview, we emphasize primarily those points on which we have our own insights to share. As mentioned above, we assume that the general course of the development of our science, as well as what is commonly discussed in this context, is known. The purpose of our discussions explains their incompleteness, and when we mention specific names, it is as sparingly as possible, only for illustration, and especially in cases where even the reader familiar with the literature might be uncertain as to the authors to whom we are referring.

We begin with the system of the classics, focusing on Adam Smith, Ricardo, and their immediate successors, without exploring the extent of their reliance on earlier authors. It is important to remember this system for two reasons. First, it serves as the starting point for most approaches, and its consideration is essential to understanding them. Second, it continues to exert a significant influence today, as many contemporary economists stand on its ground. Let us now turn to the first point, which gives us a perspective on the development of our science.

Natura non facit saltum – Marshall prominently placed this phrase at the head of his work as a guiding principle, and it indeed aptly characterizes

DOI: 10.4324/9781032627021-3

his approach. However, I would argue against him that the development of human culture, especially that of knowledge, proceeds in leaps and bounds. There are sudden starts and periods of stagnation; lofty hopes alternate with bitter disappointments; and even though the new builds on the old, progress is not steady. This is a well-known phenomenon in our science.

The freshness of the young day lies over the works of the classics. What a wealth of facts, results, and starting points – many of which have not yet been fully exploited – the *Wealth of Nations* offers us! Many rushed forward without checking the reliability of the path, ruthlessly exploiting these new intellectual territories. The new ideas – often distorted and inappropriately generalized – reached the widest circles. Naturally, disillusionment followed, leading to a situation that bears a striking resemblance to an economic crisis: Exhaustion replaced productivity, and excessive suspicion replaced unconditional trust. The most telling feature of this situation is not the attitude of the wider public toward economics but the internal state of the discipline. Suddenly, its development came to a halt; it seemed as if its terrain had been exhausted, as if there was nothing more to be gained from it, despite obvious shortcomings that invited further work. However, there were no workers available for the task. The edifice of economics was half built and half in ruins when powerful opponents arose. I cannot explain this peculiar stagnation, these "Hippocratic" characteristics of the economic literature roughly between 1830 and 1870. But the fact seems to me to be quite indisputable, although, to my knowledge, it has never been emphasized. Any connoisseur of literature will agree with this observation: The classical system did not succumb to external enemies – any more than the decline of societies in general can be satisfactorily attributed to external enemies – but to an internal torpor. The Historical School stormed a fortress defended by invalids. The works of the "epigones" would have been of little value even if the historical approach had never existed. It cannot be denied that some progress was made during this period: Almost every author contributed one detail or another. But the creative energy had dried up. This is especially true of J. St. Mill, as much as it pains me to judge an individual so quickly. There were indeed some promising beginnings, but it is indicative of the paralysis of economics that they were largely overlooked. I cannot find a more apt expression to characterize my impression of the literature of this period than "being at a dead end." Perhaps Smith and Ricardo themselves had reached a point where they did not know what to do next. In any case, their "epigones" were indeed at that point. Their approach had run its course, and no one knew what could replace it. It was quite understandable that what was true for one way of looking at things was applied to the economics in general, leading to the belief that its future could not be promising. Some saw their system as complete and finished, which is always a cause for concern; others felt a general sense of unease without knowing what to do next. This situation became very clear at the celebration of the centenary of *The Wealth of Nations* at the Political

Economy Club in London. In fact, the year 1876 already belonged to the new period. But the works of the innovators had not yet been noticed, and the calm of death seemed to lie over our discipline. How aptly did Mr. Lowe, who opened the debate, express this mood when he said, among other things: "I am not sanguine as to any very large or any very startling development of political economy. I observe that the triumphs which have been gained have been rather in demolishing that which has been found to be undoubtedly bad and erroneous, than in establishing new truth; and imagine that before we can attain new results, we must be furnished from without with new truths, to which our principles can be applied ... The great work has been done." What does this mean, other than that economics was exhausted, that it was no longer capable of accomplishing anything worthwhile out of itself, and that one had to look beyond its boundaries if one wanted to discover anything interesting? The only ones who demonstrated self-confidence and creative enthusiasm and who confidently looked to the future were the "historians," led by Cliffe Leslie. One newspaper aptly summed up the general mood when it suggested that this gathering was more like a funeral than a jubilee of economics.

Economics, having lost its inner vitality, was all the more diminished in its external influence because, during its ascent, it had ventured far too deeply into the realm of practical problems, giving superficial and general answers to questions which were too complex to be solved at the first attempt. As stone after stone fell from the scientific edifice (wage-fund theory, population theory, etc.), practical results were repeatedly contradicted by facts. So much had been heard about economics, its pretensions were so great, and the misuse of science so obvious that people turned their backs on it.

Thus, the historical approach gained considerable ground: People began to abandon theories that could prove everything and nothing, frozen in empty phrases, and began to focus on the accumulation of facts and the practical issues of social and economic policy. This success was not total, however. The fact that the old classical arguments were still invoked in discussions of current issues and that the Free Trade Party and the Manchester School did not want to abandon these theories that were favorable to them would have been of little significance for science as such. But many academic economists also clung to the theory. For a while, they could console themselves with the hope that it would be swept away by the tide of time. This hope did not materialize. Instead, a new energy stirred in the ruins, and the horde of theorists began to renew itself, to multiply, and soon to counterattack. The historians did not immediately realize that they were now facing different adversaries, and categorized them along with the remaining epigones of the classics. It was not the latter, however, but the new combatants who reignited the familiar methodological dispute [Methodenstreit]. It was a mistake to confront them with the same arguments used against the classics. But they invited this upon themselves by showing a propensity to take over the legacy of the classics.

The reader knows which group of economists we are talking about: Menger, Jevons, Walras, and their successors. Their position was challenging at first. A period of neglect was followed by a period of struggle and misunderstanding. The theory had been shelved, and there was no inclination to take it up again. But the new approach held its own and made even greater strides. Today, we can say that we are witnessing a resurgence of theory. Admittedly, the classical system has not gained much from it; rather, it has experienced a new attack that has completely shaken it.

To understand this situation, one must have a clearer idea of the nature and content of what we have called the classical system than is generally the case. The first thing that strikes me about the work of the classics is that it is composed of quite different elements. It is astonishing how little attention has been paid to this, and it seems that a crucial reason for the partial inconclusiveness of the methodological dispute lies in the fact that the methods were not sufficiently differentiated, trying to apply to the whole arguments that could only apply to one of its parts. The legacy of the classics consists of a scientific component and a political component. It is not an exaggeration to say that the great success and the great defeat of the classical system came much more from the latter than from the former.

Free trade and laissez-faire were the rallying cries of the first half of the 19th century, and the reaction against them, as well as against the practical implications of other theories such as wage theory, was primarily directed by the onslaught of the historical and the newer socio-political approaches. These circles were not interested in actual economic theory. Nevertheless, it was tacitly assumed that the same theory fell with these practical assertions and excesses. Now, this is decidedly incorrect. They are by no means the inevitable consequence of the purely economic arguments of the classics and can be separated from them. It would not be difficult to prove this. For example, it is easy to see that the theoretical content of Ricardo's chapter on wages does not necessarily lead to what the author calls "poor-laws." If the latter is rejected, the former remains valid. And it is only the scientific legacy of the classics that really counts. But even that is not entirely homogeneous. Economics is its most important and valuable part. But it also includes philosophies on individualism and collectivism, on the factors that determine human actions, etc. Everything that does not belong to economics will be shown later. We can and must admit that the attacks here were justified. But that is all; the pure economics of the classics, paradoxical as it may sound, remained largely untouched by the historical onslaught. One did not even examine it, contenting oneself with condemning it wholesale, along with other elements with which it seemed to be mixed. It was the advocates of the new theory who examined classical economics. Did they dismantle it and replace it with something new? This is a question that can be answered in many different ways. We do not want to answer it here; the following discussions provide an answer in their entirety. However, we do not want to hide our opinion:

Yes, the system of modern theory is essentially new, and even the results that agree with those of the classical system are derived by different means. Undoubtedly, we owe a whole arsenal of concepts and ideas to the classics, and certainly the new theory would not be possible without the old, but the latter is just as "outdated" as the older literature of any other science. This view seems to me nothing more than natural and equidistant from all the extremes that are so often expressed.

The preceding remarks should provide the foundation for a brief description of the current factions in our field. As we have already seen and will soon see again, almost all its directions can trace their origins back to the classics. Whether one followed their paths and further developed their methods, or criticized them and tried to replace what was rejected, whether one admired them or attacked them, the starting point was always the classics. One might be inclined to deny this; each new direction strives to stand on its own and more or less strongly rejects association with older works, and yet, such an association exists. The Historical School began with a critique of classical results. The classics provided it with its terminology and economic conceptual framework, and classical ideas can be found both consciously and unconsciously expressed in the works of this approach. It goes without saying that the same is even more true of the new theory.

As a result, we can observe a clear progression in our discipline, even if it has not been straightforward, consistent, and calm. Like the tributaries of a river delta, the individual paths originate from a common source and are organically connected. One often hears the claim that German economics in particular has lost touch with the classics. This is certainly not true as far as theory is concerned; to the extent that theory is pursued at all in Germany, the classics are given their due. They also exert a quiet but profound influence beyond pure theory.

The economist who deals in his "Introduction" with the various branches of economics usually distinguishes between pure theory, which he calls "exact," "speculative," or "deductive" according to his point of view, and then, above all, between economic history and economic description, and tries to characterize them with a few general remarks. This is quite inadequate, because there are so many different tendencies within the theory that an overall judgment about them can only be expressed in the most general terms. For this reason, we wish to distinguish carefully between the various groups.

In our opinion, the classical system is the common cradle of all branches of economics, at least from a purely scientific point of view. And we believe we have done it justice. Not one of its components can be fully maintained today, but each of them has contributed to the present state of science. However, the classics are still a living force today, more so than in any other science. Many a competent mathematician has never read Newton or Laplace. That is not possible in our field. Even today, many people go back to A. Smith or Ricardo. The reason is that in our field, there is not much agreement about what our classics still teach us today and how they are to be understood, whereas in other sciences, the valuable components of the older works live on in the newer ones in a generally accepted form. But there is another reason. Other circles, which are not devoid of any understanding of theory, find it difficult to grasp the modern system, whose scientific framework is much more difficult to access, while they can follow the explanations of the classics with advantage and find them much more satisfying because they can obtain brief answers to pressing practical questions. Thus, not only the layman but also the economist often still prefers to turn to the classics rather than the moderns. Therefore, if we have first recognized the importance of the classics for the development of our science, and thus indirectly for the present, we must also include them among the modern trends: They are still alive today.

[...]

3.2 Methodological Individualism

We have cleared the way for the ambiguities surrounding the value hypothesis and the question of the motives of human action. What remains is to justify our starting point: The individual's ownership of goods. We must be prepared to face some opposition because, as we know, the individualist approach is today often considered erroneous. Atomism is one of the most common targets of the theory's critics. The classical view was based on the individual, a premise that newer economics has largely followed, making it susceptible to the same criticisms that were originally aimed at the former. Critics of the theory are often unaware of the substantial differences between the old and new economic systems on this point and generally direct their arguments against both without distinction. The theorists have certainly responded, giving rise to one of those controversies that exhibit the inconclusiveness characteristic of many discussions of fundamental issues in our discipline. Both sides put forward general arguments and defend them with a determination shaped by the political and social scope they ascribe to them. Naturally, no agreement can ever be reached in this way, and often it seems that no agreement is even sought. In order to clarify the situation, however, nothing more is needed than a calm consideration of the problems and goals to which the conflicting views actually relate. Once this is done, the dispute loses its distasteful nature, and the challenges seem to resolve themselves. This is what we want to do, without haste. First, we will examine the criticisms of the individualist perspective by the theory's opponents, and then we will explore the various currents within the theory itself that pursue the same goal.

What did the critics of the classical system have in mind when they attacked its individualist foundation? Like almost all attacks against the classical system, this one was directed primarily against certain points of contention in the practical sphere. Individualism is in varying degrees opposed to socialism and to any form of social policy; the slogans of "free play of economic forces," "individual initiative and responsibility" were opposed by other slogans. The political downfall of individualistic liberalism also damaged the scientific credibility of works in which individualist principles were apparently combined with the foundations of pure economics. All this is well known. It is also well known how the tremendous development of socio-political endeavors, in which scientific circles played such a prominent role, led to a vehement opposition to individualism on both ethical and political grounds. The importance of the individuals was downplayed: They were reminded that they owed their existence and development to society, and that the fruits of their labor did not belong to them alone.

But enough of that. There is no doubt that much of the hostility toward atomism in economics stems from the tendency just discussed. However, it is important to understand that there is absolutely no connection between individualist science and political individualism. The attacks of historians and social politicians on the individualistic political economists may be justified; some of them certainly are, and when the historian criticizes the political statement of the theorist, he is right to do so; such a statement would not be tenable if the theorists had paid more attention to history. But it would be going too far to blame the field of social economics for that. The theory talks a lot about free competition and says that, up to a certain point, this would lead to the greatest possible satisfaction of the economic actor. However, this assertion, correctly formulated, is no longer open to criticism and loses all practical interest, as we will see later. It is impossible to derive from the theory an argument for or against political individualism. Those who deny such a possibility are quite right, and we agree with them in opposing its misuse to justify indifference to social misery. But they are wrong to reject the theory on this ground.

To summarize this part of our argument: We must make a clear distinction between political individualism and methodological individualism. They have absolutely nothing in common. The former is based on general principles, such as the idea that freedom contributes more than anything else to the development of the individual and to the well-being of society as a whole, and makes a whole series of claims; the latter does nothing of the sort, makes no claims, and has no specific presuppositions. It simply means that when we describe certain economic processes, we must base them on the actions of individuals. The question now is whether this starting point is useful and sufficiently far-reaching, or whether, given some specific problems and the field of social economics as a whole, it would be more appropriate to take society as the starting point. But this is merely a methodological question. Socialists can answer it by relying on methodological individualism, and political individualists by relying on a social approach, without contradicting themselves. In this way, we have achieved something: We have stripped our question of its practical implications and the crown of thorns of immediate interest. This has already been done to some extent in the newer economics, and therein lies a great — perhaps the greatest — difference between the modern and the older system. In the latter, it is often difficult to distinguish pure theory from practical judgment, though it is usually possible to do so; the former tries to keep itself free from digressions,[2] and some theorists have vigorously rejected association with "Manchesterism." Admittedly, this principle is often breached, and here the opponents are right, but on the whole, the science may be regarded as freed from this hindrance.

Now we turn to the second part of our task. We must admit that our capacity at this stage is limited to demonstrating our understanding of the objections raised and expressing our thoughts on them; a complete answer to the whole question can only be given by the totality of our discussions. Replacing the individual approach with a social one, or at least paying more attention to the social dimension, is one of the most frequently expressed desires. If one were to ask for the most urgent reform in our field, this point would always be mentioned, among others. But how should this be done, and what would be the benefits?

It seems to us that this tendency grows to a large extent out of the one just discussed. The social politician and the economist are often one and the same person. If the former attaches great importance to social questions, it is natural that the latter should do the same. Let us remember what has been said, namely that this connection is not necessary. But we cannot simply dismiss the scientific approach of this group; we must examine it on its own merits. Moreover, both biology and sociology put forward ideas that point in the same direction. Some biologists speak of an "erreur individualiste," which would consist in the tendency to consider the individual in too much isolation, when he is nothing more than a link in the chain of a long development. Similarly, some economists argue that an individualist economics is of little value on the premise that individuals cannot exist in isolation and can only be understood within their social milieu, and that they are subject to myriad social influences that cannot possibly be studied at the individual level. Many sociologists have expressed similar views. Biology has also exerted a more direct influence, primarily through the channel of the so-called organic conception of the state, though this is less relevant here. Finally, the third element of the discussed tendency comes from certain theorists who use the concepts of society and social value within pure theory. Let us take a closer look at this. It would not be very useful for us to enter into the general discussion, which, by the way, is only too well known. For example, if we were to examine the nature of economics, we would have to align ourselves with one of the two perspectives that strongly define the opposing viewpoints in this field. These are the views of the economy as an "organism" on the one hand, and as a "result of the economic actions and being of individuals" on the other. Once again, we see that nothing is easier than defending both perspectives with broad arguments. Of course, any collective phenomenon consists of individual events, which leads to the conclusion that one must study the latter in order to understand the former. It is equally obvious that the members of a national economy, or of any category within it, are far more interconnected by innumerable ties with each other than they are with members of other national economies, so that economic (and other) effects and interdependencies, cooperation as well as antagonisms, play a crucial role that may not be immediately visible at the individual level. This, in turn, implies that one should take some social group as a starting point and unit of thought. One party can argue to the other that the state is not an animal body and that every machine is made up of distinguishable components, just as effectively as the latter can convince the former that people never live and work in isolation and that a machine is more than the sum of unrelated pieces of metal. Once again, we would like to emphasize that analogies and broad generalizations lead nowhere: Only a detailed study can yield valuable results. However, the issue at hand is different. Namely, the nature of the economy and whether the individual is the driving force or whether such a force must be sought elsewhere are of no importance to us. We are largely willing to accept whatever social scientists and historians have to say on this point, and we do not believe it is worth our time to discuss an abstract model in terms of natural law. We fully acknowledge that social influences determine the actions of individuals and that the individual is an infinitesimal factor, but that does not matter here. What matters to us is not how these things really behave, but how we must schematize or stylize them to best serve our purposes; in other words, which conception is most convenient from the standpoint of the results of pure economics.

This statement is as paradoxical as it is fundamental: Should the nature of the national economy be irrelevant to the economist? We do not hesitate to answer in the affirmative. In fact, we would go further; we would argue that the nature of an economy itself is irrelevant to us. We must focus on our desired result, in this case the phenomenon of price determination, and draw only on what is absolutely necessary to achieve our goal. Only then can the forms of our thinking and its actual meaning emerge sharply and vividly. And we cannot say a priori what is necessary.

In light of the problem at hand, the above clarifies the nature of what we propose to call "methodological individualism." We have already noted that it makes no practical demands, nor does it make any moral or other judgments about various organizational forms of the national economy, and therefore cannot be countered by objections in this category. Moreover, we now realize that it does not assert any facts, since we make no claims about what influences people's actions. Our aim is to describe certain economic processes within very narrow limits. The deeper reasons for these processes may be interesting, but they do not affect our results. These reasons belong to the field of sociology, and therefore our results cannot be refuted by arguing that processes in an economy cannot be explained on an individual basis alone. If an economist adorns the individualist method with facts and claims, for example, that the individual is the central point of any explanation, then we cannot agree with this, and in this respect, we fully agree with the opponents.

But it must not be forgotten that very often, and even as a rule, such statements can be disregarded without altering the purely economic aspect of the question. In such cases, the criticism can easily go so far as to make it impossible to distinguish between right and wrong.

In essence, methodological individualism does not involve any philosophical speculation, future ideals, or anything similar, even though these attributes have been, to some extent, rightly and partly wrongly, ascribed to the theory as explained earlier. Any impartial observer will have to concede that our exposition does not lend itself to any of these attacks, which have become slogans and are repeated over and over again.

We are merely suggesting that the individualist approach leads quickly and efficiently to results of considerable utility and that, within the confines of pure theory, a social approach offers no substantial advantages and is therefore unnecessary. Beyond the boundaries of pure theory, things look different. In organizational theory, for example, and in sociology in general, individualism will not get you very far, but this is not particularly regrettable given its purely methodological character.

We have now taken a further step and removed some of the difficulties that often act as stumbling blocks, but we have also stripped our question of any interest beyond the purely scientific. We have not so much solved a problem as shown that we do not need to solve it. It is obvious that those theoretical discussions which employ the famous or notorious "Robinson" methods cannot be refuted by the objection that the latter can exist only in exceptional cases and only for a long time. Here, the misunderstanding inherent in many such objections becomes particularly clear.

There are no fundamental objections to "atomism" as we present it. What has been raised concerns things that may seem related to it, but can be dissociated from it. Certainly, we are not interested in individual processes as such, but they serve to describe collective phenomena in our field. The action of an individual is as indifferent to us as the color of a person's hair is to an ethnologist. However, one cannot observe the hair color of a population, only of individuals, and from those individual observations, one can somehow determine the hair color that is (statistically) typical or representative of that population. The analogy may not be perfect, but it illustrates that the individualist method and the social results are by no means incompatible.

We still believe that the old individualist method is indispensable today, but only for the purposes of pure theory in the narrowest sense. Our method is suitable only for that purpose and has produced useful results only in that field. It is neither necessary nor useful to abandon it in light of the present range of problems under investigation. Perhaps it will be necessary in the future, as is already the case outside this very narrow field. But for now, and for the foreseeable future, any further interpretation would only hinder real progress. Of course, we cannot prove this here by general reasoning; only a detailed examination of the pure theory can reveal this; each of its propositions must be examined.

All we have been able to do so far is address some objections, dispel some misunderstandings, and assure the reader that we do not intend to do anything that might raise fundamental concerns. Only such issues could be discussed in general terms. From now on, we will generally refrain from discussing social categories and instead show that the individualist approach, free of any practical interest, is valid and sufficient in our context. This second part of our proof, therefore, only follows from the totality of what comes next. Everyone is free to formulate economic concepts of a social category for the purpose of discussing social or political problems, wherever this may be desirable. We emphasize again and again that what has been said applies only to the system of theory in its purest form.

At this point, we would like to mention the two main groups of terms that have been used to introduce the social dimension and that we would like to reject for the reasons already explained. The first is characterized by terms such as "national income," "national wealth," "social capital," and plays a role especially in German literature (Held, Wagner). Stolzmann, in particular, argues for the necessity of their introduction. But nothing speaks so much in our favor as the fact that he actually makes little use of them in purely theoretical questions, and where he does, they are only a mode of expression and do not change the individualist basis of the theory.

If one constructs the framework of our theory without any external prejudices or demands, these concepts do not arise at all. Therefore, we will not deal with them further, but if we did, it would become clear that they are fraught with a multitude of ambiguities and complexities and that they are closely tied to many misconceptions, without even leading to a truly valuable statement.

The second group is rooted in the concept of social value. There are echoes of this in the earliest stages of the theory, but it has gained fundamental importance only in the present, namely in the concept of "social value" of the American authors. Some of the concepts of this group have no application at all, such as "value to mankind," which itself has no precise meaning [more on this in my article "On the Concept of Social Value" in the *Quarterly Journal of Economics*, 1908]. Only the social value of the Clark School has any real scientific meaning. Even this we cannot discuss here, except to point out that we can ignore it for methodological purposes.

We should note one more thing. We often encounter the terms "total demand" and "total supply." These are not social categories but merely aggregations of individual processes. We do not believe that by using them, we meet the requirement to consider the social dimension. To do so would be to view social phenomena as merely the sum of individual phenomena, a perspective that we explicitly reject. These concepts have a completely individual basis.

Notes

1 From: Schumpeter, J. A. (1908). *Das Wesen und der Hauptinhalt der theoretischen Nationalökonomie* [*The Nature and Essence of Economic Theory*]. Leipzig: Verlag von Duncker. "By way of introduction," § II, pp. 7–16 and Chapter VI. "Methodological individualism," pp. 89–98.
2 Translator's note: The original text seems to contain a mistake, which was corrected here (inversion between *the former* and *the latter*).

4 Georg Simmel (1905-1907)

The intrinsic conditions of historical knowledge and the mental nature of history[1]

4.1 Foreword to the third edition

The subject of this book is the question of how the material of immediate experience is transformed into the theoretical structure we call history. It aims to show that this transformation is more radical than naive consciousness tends to assume. Consequently, it critiques historical realism, which sees the science of history as the reproduction of what happened "as it really was"; historical realism seems to make the same mistake as artistic realism, which attempts to copy reality without recognizing how profoundly this "copying" already stylizes its content. Although the power of the knowing mind to shape the data of experience is generally recognized in relation to nature, it is obviously more difficult to recognize it in relation to history since its material is already of a psychic nature. When this material is transformed into history, the categories brought into play, their overall autonomy, and the material's compliance with their demands do not stand out as clearly from the material itself as they do in the natural sciences. The question raised here therefore concerns the a priori of historical knowledge, which cannot be examined in detail but only in principle. In the face of historical realism, for which events are reproduced in history as they happened and at most with a quantitative compression, we must assert our right to ask in the Kantian sense: How is history possible?

The philosophical value of Kant's answer to the question, "How is nature possible? - lies in the freedom it grants to the self in relation to raw nature. Certainly not with regard to its arbitrariness and individual fluctuations, but with regard to its essence and its necessities, which are not imposed from outside but constitute its immediate life. Thus, of the two aggressions that threaten the modern subject – by nature and by history – one is abolished. Nature, because its mechanism subjects the mind to the same blind compulsion as the falling stone and the growing stem, and history, because it reduces the mind to a mere intersection of the social threads that run through history, dissolving all its activity into the administration of the species' heritage.

Since Kant, the autonomy of the mind has dominated the natural determinisms to which our empirical existence is subject. The conscious representation

DOI: 10.4324/9781032627021-4

of nature, the understanding of its forces, and what it can be for the mind are all achievements of the mind itself. However, the enslavement of the self by nature, once abolished by the mind, has been transformed into the enslavement of the mind by the mind itself. Individualities dissolved into history, which is the history of the mind, while the necessity and domination exercised over them still seemed to be freedom. In reality, however, history, as a given, as a reality, and as a supra-personal power, is no less an aggression of the self by a non-self. The temptation to confuse what is actually enslavement to a foreign being with freedom is more subtle here because what binds us in this case shares the same substantial essence as ourselves. The liberation that Kant achieved from naturalism is also needed from historicism. It is possible that in both cases, the same critique of knowledge applies, namely that the mind forms the representation of mental existence, which we call history, just as sovereignly and solely through its own specific categories of knowledge. The individual as object of knowledge is a product of nature and history, but it is the individual as knowing subject that creates nature and history. The conscious form of mental reality that we call history, which results from the activity of each individual, itself exists only as a product of the formative activity of the self. It is the mind itself that gives a shore and a rhythm to the flow of becoming and transforms this flow into history. The general perspective that guides the specificity of the following analyses can therefore be described as the preservation of the freedom of the mind and its creative power against historicism, as Kant did against naturalism.

The second edition of this book is a new work compared to the first, both in orientation and execution. The third edition does not introduce any major changes. However, apart from some minor corrections, a number of additions have been made. Their purpose is not to extend the theory developed here to a wider range of phenomena but rather to reveal the unity of the philosophical principle underlying the individual reflections and observations at increasingly deeper levels.

4.2 The mental nature of history

If the theory of knowledge in general starts from the fact that knowledge is a representation and its subject is mental, the theory of historical knowledge is further characterized by the fact that its objects are also the knowing, willing, and feeling of personalities, that its objects are psychical beings. All observable processes, political and social, economic and religious, legal and technical, would be neither interesting nor comprehensible to us if they did not arise from mental processes and give rise to mental processes. If history is not to be a puppet show, then it is the history of mental processes, and all the external events it describes are nothing more than the bridges between the impulses and acts of will on the one hand, and the emotional reactions triggered by those events on the other. Attempts to trace the specific manifestations of historical events back to physical conditions do not change this. The nature of soil and climate would remain as irrelevant to the course of history as the soil and climate of Sirius if they did not directly and indirectly affect the psychological condition of peoples.

[…]

4.3 Nomological regularities and individuality

[…]

Before going further into psychological reality as the substance of history, we must first establish the methodological relationship between psychology and history. It is undeniable that all processes that interest us in the traditional sense of history are mental processes. Even material processes, such as the building of St. Peter's or the digging of the Gotthard tunnel, are of interest to the historian only as manifestations of mental events, or more precisely, as the meeting points of intentional, intellectual, or emotional series. The mere interest in a mental process, however, is not in itself a psychological interest. For psychology, a process is essential merely because it is mental; it has no interest in the contents of consciousness conveyed by mental energy. Of course, we only know the process through the contents that exist or have existed in consciousness, but the essential interest of psychology lies in the dynamics of going back and forth between these contents. The contents would be indifferent if they could be detached from their creation or realization by the psychic energies, as happens within the logical, scientific, or metaphysical considerations, which for this very reason form the antipole of psychology.

History, on the other hand, is less interested in the development of psychological content than in the psychological development of content. For history, each piece of content is fixed at a certain point in time; it is the process that has made it possible and that makes it comprehensible at that moment that is naturally of the greatest importance – not in and for itself, but because it is the producer of those factual contents of practical or intellectual, religious or artistic consciousness that make up the historical series. History, therefore, is a kind of mediator between the purely logical or factual analysis of our mental contents and psychology, which considers the changes of mental contents only from a dynamic point of view. What is important for history is the factual content, but in its movement and mental becoming. Each of these sciences emphasizes an aspect of the unity of being and becoming of the mind, which we experience directly but cannot fully grasp intellectually. In order to approach this unity analytically, we divide it into two concepts: process and content. From this, the scientific division of labor has created psychology, which focuses on processes and their factual regularities; logic and the empirical sciences, which concentrate on content and disregard processes; and, finally, history, which, as we shall see, defines its objects only by virtue of their factual importance and significance and focuses on certain contents selected for their essential character in the course of the development in which they are produced by the mental process.

4.4 The psychological a priori and its antithetical consequences

Whatever the scientific category to which knowledge of the inner nature of historical events may belong, the fact that it is the starting point and goal of all descriptions of their outer nature requires a set of special presuppositions that the epistemology of history must uncover.

Kant assigned to the formative activity of the mind an unprecedentedly expanded sphere of power in relation to all the given "material" of the imagination. Where the naive view sees knowledge as a process by which things would come to irradiate a passive subject, Kant sees the function of the intellect as structuring all knowledge by providing its a priori forms. However, this extension of form can become a restriction of substance if we forget that the mental functions that Kant describes as the a priori of knowledge are valid only in the realm of the natural sciences. We might wonder whether subjective experience is not "possible" only under a priori conditions that are absent from the Kantian system, whether, for example, the causal relation by which we understand the emergence of one idea as the consequence of another is not fundamentally different from that which explains the causation of one physical movement by another.

It is much more important to note that the Kantian a priori, which "makes experience possible in general," is only the highest degree in a series whose lower degrees descend deeply into the particular domains of experience. As seen from above, certain propositions appear empirical, that is, they represent an application of the most general forms of thought to particular materials. But these propositions can function as a priori for whole provinces of knowledge. They then function as forms of connection at the service of that particular faculty of the mind, which, by arranging, tuning, and emphasizing, can pour the data of experience into the most diverse definite forms.

This connecting activity, which is reflected in the use of a priori propositions, generally remains unconscious because consciousness is more attentive to the external information it examines than to its own internal activity. Since these a priori propositions are uniformly applied to the most diverse contents, they lead to an effect of habituation due to their permanence and intrinsic generality. Consciousness then tends to glide over these propositions as if they were absolutely self-evident. It is also true here that what comes first in the rational order – the cognitive function of the mind – is often the last thing we pay attention to or observe. Because of his sharp separation between a priori and empirical knowledge, Kant did not fully recognize the extent of the unconscious domination of forms of connection over factual material. Of course, this separation remains perfectly justified from the point of view of methods, principles, and categories, and the discussion concerns only the content of the functions called a priori. But it will probably be shown that certain propositions, which already appear empirical from Kant's single elevated point of view, still have, for special branches of knowledge, the full formative power of the a priori.

Today, by letting the experience reach much higher than Kant did, the a priori reaches much lower for us. By a series of imperceptible transitions, we pass from the most general forms, those that apply to all empirical data and to every singular experience, to specific forms which, though of empirical origin, can be used as a priori for certain contents. Such a transition can be observed when, in a certain area of life or in a certain science, the principle of causality is applied or when different objects that are assumed to be identical are brought together under a common concept. Another example would be that any law, in the legal sense of the word, implies that a certain state of affairs is considered desirable. The principle that this state of affairs can only be achieved through the introduction of norms and sanctions capable of regulating social relations is a very general a priori, which leads to a certain shaping, that is, the connection of pre-existing representations. But this form of connection for the formation of laws is not as general as, for example, the cause-and-effect relationship introduced between motivations and behavior. This relationship establishes a connection between phenomena that cannot be discerned from the phenomena themselves. Of course, it is also indispensable for lawmaking. The a priori that constitute the form of the law must be regarded as general in relation to the more specific propositions that are implemented for certain aspects of the legislation.

For example, the principle that the burden of proof lies with the plaintiff, or the principles that delimit the scope of the common law, allow for a shaping of the facts for the purpose of knowing what is right – a shaping that does not lie in the facts themselves but only in an interpretation of them.

All human interaction at all times relies on the assumption that certain physical movements of each individual, such as gestures, facial expressions, and sounds, are based on mental processes of an intellectual, emotional, or volitional nature. Thus, we understand what is inside only by analogy with what is outside, as language already indicates, since words borrowed from the world of external perception are used to characterize all mental processes. On the other hand, we understand external human behavior only by projecting internal states onto it. The mixture between experience and its spontaneous extrapolation, manifested in this way, is easy to understand: The experience we have of our own selves reveals to us the connection between internal processes and their expressions, which allows us to infer from the same process observed in others a mental event similar to our own.

The correspondence we thus establish between our mental life and that of others, inferred on the basis of their observable behavior, must always remain a hypothesis, and this, by its function, constitutes an a priori on which any practical or cognitive relationship between one subject and another is based. If we were to say that experience has convinced us of the correctness of this hypothesis, and to confirm it every time we observe the same behavior in others, we would then be running around in circles. For, on the one hand, we would never arrive at such an assumption if this correspondence were not already presupposed and, on the other hand, all experience as such only leads to an increasing certainty that certain observable behaviors are always followed by certain others. The intermediate link that connects them lies in a mental process that is not accessible to experience.

And now we not only interpret this single perceived action or speech through a corresponding mental basis, but we construct an in principle uninterrupted mental series with innumerable links which have no direct external counterpart; we impute this series or these many series to an overall character of the personality; we interpret outwardly identical processes by manifold, often mutually opposed psychological ones; and by no means only where we suspect lies and dissimulation. These additional psychological hypotheses allow us to supplement the initial interpretations associated with our immediate perceptions. Without them, the actions of others would be nothing more to us than a meaningless and incoherent jumble of erratic impulses.

When we speak of a priori conceptions, we tend to focus on the content of the thought, which stands in the whole experience as coordinated with the sensually given, and to overlook that the a priori, which can be expressed in propositional forms, is itself only the formulation of inner energies that transform the given sensual material into an object of knowledge. The a priori plays a dynamic role in our way of thinking. It is a function whose reality is manifested or solidified in its final objective result, which is cognition. However, the significance of the a priori does not derive from the logical content of the concepts in which it is subsequently expressible, but from its fundamental role in shaping our cognitive world. In this sense, the notion that another's mind is a coherent unit for us, that is, that it represents an intelligible collection of interconnected processes that allow us to recognize it, constitutes an a priori. The function of this a priori is to fill in the gaps of mental phenomena that lie behind what is observable, but it also goes beyond that. We ourselves supplement the observable in order to meet the demands of this internal connection, or to ensure that there is an internal connection at all.

Even with the utmost care for the truth, the narrators add to their direct observations elements that complete the event in the sense they infer from what is actually given. Similarly, listeners, depending on their experiences and the impact of those experiences on their imagination, always envision more in their minds than what is explicitly conveyed to them. Sensory physiology demonstrates with countless examples that we unconsciously fill in the gaps of partial sensory impressions related to individual objects or movements based on our prior experiences. The same is true for complex events. We supplement the observed data with mental hypotheses, according to our experience, about the continuity and progression of mental life, the correlation of its internal energies, or the unfolding of intentional processes. These hypotheses are not only prompted by external observations, but in accordance with the laws of experience regarding the connection between the internal and the external, they supplement the observable events to such an extent that they form an unbroken series parallel to the internal processes.

The fact that external information can be spontaneously supplemented in this way is one of the most incontrovertible proofs that internal processes are not simply deduced from observable facts but are added to those facts on the basis of general assumptions. In everyday life, too, there are numerous opportunities to verify the validity of this a priori and the specific consequences that flow from it, since the actions we take are always a response to the anticipated external behavior of others. When it comes to more abstract and complex mental processes, however, these conclusions become uncertain, leading to many errors and showing that even in the least ambiguous cases, they are only assumptions. If they appear to be reliable guides, it is because of their usefulness for knowledge and action, not because of any logical necessity that would make them follow rationally from what is really given.

These presuppositions of everyday life are more prevalent and influential in historical research than in any other field, although they are often introduced in an uncontrolled and unsystematic manner. Even assuming that we could interpret and supplement factual data without hesitation, determining their meaning would be a considerable task in itself. However, the undertaking becomes remarkably more subtle and challenging because, as we can easily observe, the same inner event can be associated with different external consequences. It is only by comparing the mental correlates or outcomes that potentially accompany that first event that we can understand how the same event must be placed under the authority of either a given psychological norm or an opposing one.

Consider, for example, Sybel's account of the relations between the Committee of Public Safety and the Hebertists in 1793 (*History of the Revolution*, II, 364):

Hitherto they [the Hebertists] had enjoyed excellent relations with Robespierre: he had relied on the force they represented, and had consequently furthered their aims; but what was to irrevocably separate them was simply the fact that Robespierre was now at the head of the highest organ of the State, while the Hebertists remained in a subordinate position.

The observable facts are these: Robespierre supports the interests of the Hebertists; they form an alliance with him. Robespierre gains a dominant position; they break the alliance. These facts form a perfectly understandable series based on certain psychological assumptions. But these presuppositions are by no means as convincing and unambiguous as they seem at first glance.

It is true that by furthering a person's goals and doing them a favor, one can often secure their affection and devotion. But the opposite can also happen.

The history of the bloody family rivalries of the Trecento provides us with an anecdote that illustrates this point. A nobleman of Ravenna had gathered all his enemies in one house and could have killed them without further ado; instead, he let them go and gave them rich gifts. Afterwards, they became more aggressive and cunning toward him, constantly trying to destroy him because, according to the story, the shame of the good that had befallen them did not leave them at peace.

Again, the sequence of external events is quite understandable, provided that an intermediate psychological assumption is introduced, namely, that a benefit can affect the recipient's sense of personal integrity, eat away at him, and make him an enemy of his benefactor. For our purposes, it is indifferent whether in the present example direct statements of the participants have been handed down, which spare the historians their own psychological construction, for not only can they not do without such construction in the face of the innumerable accounts of purely external events, but they can accept the direct statements of the actors about their mental states only under one condition: They must find these psychological states plausible and be able to reconstruct them in the light of their own experience.

We can understand that the elevation of Robespierre to the position of head of government could have provoked hostile reactions from the Hebertists only if we accept that it aroused hatred and envy in them. But we would also find it plausible that the same facts could have produced the opposite results. We would have easily understood that once Robespierre's powerful personality seemed to have succeeded and he had achieved a dominant position, all resistance, even internal, was broken. We would have understood that the feeling of not being able to oppose this power led his rivals to submit, and that by swearing allegiance to Robespierre, they sought to share his power. The psychological hypotheses of this order allow us to understand the Roman Senate at the time of the military dictatorship. In one case, we are satisfied with the fact that generosity or accession to power had such a subsequent psychological effect of either closeness or distance, without finding the reason for this difference in the act itself as an external act. On the contrary, it is only through the subsequent events that we are informed of the psychological states responsible for this difference, but these in turn only become understandable if we relate them to the psychological states they suggest to us.

It is sometimes said that in democratic constitutions, where the government is elected in shorter periods and alternates between only two major parties, the ruling party cannot abuse its situation for fear of retaliation from the opposing party should it be relegated to opposition. In reality, however, when such a situation arises, it is often observed that the party in power ruthlessly and imprudently exploits its momentary dominance. To explain this difference in the consequences of the same external factors, we will invoke unobservable inner differences: The "character" of this or that personality or party would explain the observed difference; depending on this character, one or the other of two opposite consequences would become more likely. It should be noted, however, that this "character," whatever it may be, can only be known through its external manifestations. The mental cause of difference can never be grasped directly and always remains a hypothesis based on observable phenomena, but it shows its necessity for the understanding of phenomena in that the obvious obligation to deduce it first from these phenomena themselves, and to examine carefully all their contradictions, does not lead in any way to doubt its application and its relevance.

Let me give another example. Knapp (*The Peasants*, 82)[2] discusses the living conditions of Russian agricultural workers after the abolition of serfdom:

> The peasants agreed to perform a certain number of services for the landlord in exchange for wages. They did so reluctantly, for the changed legal basis did not console them for the fact that they were still working for the landlord; and it did not help the landlord much either, for the now negotiated instead of forced peasant service was poorly performed, despite the payment.

The first assumption takes it for granted, and in any case considers it unworthy of discussion, that the emotional response to a given situation does not change as long as the situation remains externally identical, even if, over time, it produces mental states different from those that initially triggered the observed emotional response. The second suggests that the farmer, over whom one no longer has full sovereign control and with whom one must now negotiate, works less efficiently than before. However, if the facts had shown steady economic growth in Russia after 1864, psychological reasons directly opposed to the above would have been invoked, and an equally plausible causal relationship would have been established: One would have easily seen that it is not the external action but the ethical basis, and the motive from which it is done, that determine whether work is done with desire and zeal or with contrary feelings.

With regard to forced peasant labor, Prussian history also teaches us that, in contrast to the previous case, before the abolition of serfdom, everyone complained that serfs were considered particularly inefficient, indolent, and unscrupulous.[3]

These examples are to be found in large numbers in every work of history. On the one hand, they should not lead us to an easy and unfounded skepticism about psychological interpretation in general. On the other hand, the divergences between possible interpretations show that the problem of psychological interpretation is not without ambiguity, and that it is therefore necessary to give it some attention. These presuppositions and the importance of choosing among them are particularly evident in the many cases in which observable facts are transmitted to us in dubious or ambiguous ways, cases in which the identification and classification of facts depend on their psychological plausibility.

Even in the most obvious cases, it is not the "plain fact" that determines the comprehensibility of the result of a phenomenon. On the contrary, it is the major psychological propositions, together with the minor psychological proposition represented by the "plain fact," that make the outcome of a phenomenon seem possible and understandable. We subsume observable human actions under the unobservable intentions and feelings that are necessary to fit those actions into an intelligible scheme. If we had no way to go beyond the directly observable facts, we would have great difficulty understanding any historical development or sequence of events.

Somewhere, Helmholtz says that the proof of the principle of causality would be very weak if it were deduced from experience. Cases in which the principle can be proved are rare compared to the vast number of cases in which a complete causal account is lacking. While this proposition is already valid for infra-mental processes, it must be even more difficult to find evidence for the principle of causality when considering the causal relationships between observable phenomena and the obscure and complex brain processes that link them.

In the psychophysical parallelism hypothesis, which we will not discuss here, we would have complete knowledge if we could fully understand the external physical influences that lie between the individual acts of a historical personality, and if we knew the psychological meaning of each cerebral process involved in this sequence. This, of course, is an unattainable, perhaps even self-contradictory, ideal. Therefore, we must limit ourselves to interpreting observable processes by supplementing them with and basing them on mental processes.

4.5 Conscious and unconscious motives

The explanation of a historical process is always hypothetical, insofar as it is based on psychological statements. This hypothetical character is due, first of all, to the fact that there are equally plausible but conflicting interpretations of the processes that develop in the subject's consciousness. But the ambiguity stems even more from the fact that we do not know to what extent an observable event is the result of a conscious process or, on the contrary, of unconscious forces. Especially in the case of mass movements, we can observe significant, characteristic, expedient – or also inexpedient – things happening whose conscious motivation is quite doubtful.

The mystery of unconscious mental processes arises in the following way: We observe actions that closely resemble those produced by reflection and will, but it is impossible to attribute them to conscious motives. We infer that these motives may still be present, but in an unconscious form. In fact, the notion of unconscious motivation is only a way of saying that the actual motive is unknown to us; it only indicates that we cannot identify a conscious motive. In this way, we transform a negative situation, a situation of ignorance, into a positive one. The unknown becomes the unconscious and is thus put into a certain form of mental process; this is an illusion that only satisfies the need to fill the empty causal place in human action with a psychic motive.

We observe in the life of groups instances in which the group seems to exhibit instinctive movements or reflexes similar to those of individuals. We have heard of the irrepressible tendency of some peoples to expand, to attack their neighbors, and to constantly push back their frontiers, as if driven by an instinct for expansion. We have also heard of the mysterious attraction that drove the Teutons towards Italy, similar to the instinct of migratory birds – a completely unconscious drive that leads them in certain directions.

In the interpretation of behavior, the place given to conscious reflection, to these problematic unconscious motives, or to organic types of processes, such as nervous reactions, can only be a matter of personal interpretation. One of the reasons why the boundary between conscious and unconscious motives shifts so much, leaving room for opposing interpretations, lies in the pendulum movement characteristic of mental processes. Actions that were once conscious gradually become unconscious and end up being performed in a purely mechanical way, as in the case of the pianist, who first consciously hits the key and later through a fixed mechanism of association that the image of the note excites without any intervening consciousness. Conversely, there are actions that are initially mechanical and then come under the increasingly strict control of the conscious mind, as in the case of blind instincts that give way to reflection and submission to abstract norms.

Consider the case of a group which, driven by necessity, allows itself to be deliberately drawn into a series of acts of war. It may then develop a war-like tendency for which one would search in vain for a sufficient reason in the conscience of those who act. Similarly, when one group manifests an attitude of submission and servility toward another, this may be due to perfectly conscious causes, but the causes need only persist for a time for it to become pointless to question individuals about the reasons for their attitude of submission, which now belongs to the category of reflex actions triggered by a stimulus. Obviously, we are exposed to many errors if we naively assume that the actions of individuals and groups are always the product of conscious mental processes of a teleological character.

The other case, the substitution of conscious processes for unconscious ones, needs little illustration. A high level of culture generally implies a high level of consciousness; intention replaces instinct; reflection replaces submission to mechanical influences; and affective response replaces apathetic submission. Often, a particular historical process can be described as a curve resulting from the action of these two tendencies. Initially, instinctive behaviors may rise to the level of clear consciousness and then fall back to the level of purely mechanical exercises. In the same way, the practice of an art may begin as purely instinctual and later become a conscious technique, but after a long period of practice, the master may find it to be something completely instinctual, applied without further reflection.

These two tendencies can undoubtedly be identified in the course of a group's life, making it impossible to determine objectively which aspect of its activities should be considered conscious and to what extent. The decision on this point depends on a question of principle: Should group movements be derived as a composite of individual processes, or should they be traced back to manifestations of a supra-individual group mind? Are single, dominant personalities, the real agents of collective action, or do the undifferentiated masses act on their own impulses? If we take the former view that motivation is individual, then we will ascribe a more decisive role to consciousness in explaining observable events than would be the case if we treated groups as collective subjects. To describe great men as "the consciousness of their time" is to choose between these interpretations.

A completely different understanding of the plain facts, therefore, will result, even in the case of insufficient information, in different extrapolations and assumptions, depending on whether the psychological interpretations and hypotheses introduced appeal to the clear motivations of individuals or, on the contrary, to obscure mass instincts.

In addition to this distinction between conscious individuality and unconscious masses, there is another important notion to take into account from the point of view of interpreting history: That of impersonal forces that can be the cause or effect of the actions of individuals or the situations in which they find themselves. Law and morals, language and thought, culture and forms of social interaction are undoubtedly partly the product of the intentional activities of individuals. However, the individual actors are not aware of the effect of the composition that results from these individual contributions, that is, the development of the social form that emerges from this individual raw material. In their relations with others, individuals seek only to express their affection or aloofness, indifference or interest, in the best possible way; in so doing, they help to shape the forms of social interaction. Religious concerns lead people to make statements or perform actions that they believe are the surest bridge to the divine principle, and thus they build the edifice of religious worship – a bridge to God. In business activities, they seek to protect themselves from possible abuses by taking certain precautions, thus establishing the general usages of commerce.

Every human relationship and every act of self-interest, unless it is purely self-destructive, thus contributes to the formation of the public spirit, insofar as its effects are distilled through a multitude of tiny channels whose existence escapes individual consciousness. The saying that no weaver knows what he weaves is especially true of the fabric of social life. It is true that more advanced social forms emerge only from beings capable of intentionality, but they emerge, so to speak, on the margins of individual conscious goals and without being intended by those individuals. Once developed, they act upon individuals. They represent for them mental entities that possess an ideal existence beyond and independent of their consciousness, and are a readily available common good, accessible to all, parts of which anyone can use at will. This kind of process can be interpreted in different ways. On the one hand, it can be seen as the product of action and individual consciousness, but it can also be seen as external to consciousness. The difficulty in deciding this question increases the moment these transindividual entities appear to be endowed with their own potential for change and development.

Let us consider the theory of economic forces of production, which either adequately fulfill the respective forms of production or exceed them and cause them to fall apart. This theory places the relations between purely material conditions above the knowledge and will of individuals. According to it, social forms develop completely independently of the consciousness and aspirations of individuals. They may facilitate or complicate the process, but they cannot initiate or stop it. If, therefore, the slave economy has given way to the feudal economy and the latter to wage labor, and if socialism will "develop" out of the latter, the explanatory causes of these changes are not to be sought in the consciousness of the actors themselves, but in the logical consequences, so to speak, of the state of technology at a given stage, of the productive forces developed by it, and of the constitution of the society in which these are expressed with mechanical necessity. As we can see, consciousness, which in other and more specific fields interposes itself between external events and makes them comprehensible in the first place, is completely excluded from this type of analysis. In reality, historians use both types of approaches in a relatively uncontrolled manner. The question of the extent to which consciousness is present in such a sequence of observable events is therefore generally left unresolved. The essential problem of any historical interpretation is thus left to the intuitive or doctrinal prejudices of the interpreter.

A descriptive theory of historical knowledge based on the work of historians would therefore have to determine in which cases and to what extent interpreters use consciousness as an explanatory principle, and in which cases they dispense with it in favor of obscure instincts and unconscious motives, or even autonomous sequences of purely external events. It would also have to determine the extent to which the type of interpretation chosen depends on the interpreter's own worldview. Finally, it would have to examine the extent to which, in principle and depending on the nature of the problems under consideration, these approaches actually meet the requirements inherent in the notion of explanation.

[...]

4.6 The concept of historical understanding: reconstruction by the historian of the subjectivity of the actor

If the events studied in history presuppose mental foundations, whether conscious or unconscious, then identifying their contents poses further epistemological problems. Again, we are dealing with a very general hypothesis. Whether the psychological connections that the historian makes to the events are objectively true, that is, whether they really trace the mental acts of the acting persons, would be of no interest to us if we did not understand the meaning and consequences of these processes. In the absence of this phenomenon of understanding, the validity of these psychological hypotheses could be established in many ways. Sometimes it does not need to be established by a psychological reconstruction by the historian but can be obtained directly from the statements and confessions of the historical actors. But we would not ascribe any value of truth to these hypotheses if we could not understand the mental acts that they potentially describe. But what does this understanding mean, and what are its conditions?[4]

The first condition is obvious. We must be able to reproduce in ourselves the mental acts of others. In other words, we must be able to "put ourselves in the minds of others." Understanding a spoken sentence means being able to represent in one's own mind the mental processes that inspire the speaker's words. As soon as there is an important difference between the ideas of the listener and those of the speaker, the words communicated from one to the other are not fully understood or remain completely incomprehensible. Only in the case of theoretical ideas is an immediate mental reproduction of ideas possible. In this case, it does not matter whether these ideas can be attributed to that particular individual. But they must have an identical logical form for both the speaker and the listener. When it comes to objective knowledge, I relate to the object of knowledge in exactly the same way as the person whose ideas about it I "understand": He or she merely conveys their content to me and is then, so to speak, switched off. From that moment on, the content of the ideas in question is present in my thoughts, just as it is present in the thoughts of that person. And it is neither distorted nor altered by the fact that the mental representation I have of it was originally produced by another person. In this case, a phrase like "I understand the speaker" is not entirely appropriate. It is not the speaker that I understand, but what he or she is saying.

It is quite different when the speaker's words are inspired by personal intention, prejudice, anger, fear, or irony. By recognizing this motive of the utterance, we have "understood" it in a completely different sense than by comprehending its factual content; now, attention extends beyond what is spoken to include the speaker. For historical explanation, it is the second meaning of understanding that interests us.

When I understand the content of the law of gravity or the idea of the mystical choir, I understand it as timeless. Newton and Goethe do not enter into this process of understanding as their historical creators, even though there is a complete identity between the ideas they created and those I reproduce in my mind. But as soon as I want to understand Newton's law or Goethe's verses from a historical point of view, I have to take their authors into account. There is no identity between their temporal reality and my thoughts, but an image that requires an interpretation, a selection, and a combination of individual psychological facts and facts related to the history of science and art.

The relationship we have with a mental object – a relationship which, in the case of a work of art, for example, can be of the emotional type – is, in some cases, a relationship of identity between subject and object. But when this object is considered in terms of its historical appearance or when it is treated as a historical event, this identity relationship disappears. The problem is then to confront the facts as they unfold with an intellectual representation resulting from a series of causal hypotheses, connections, analyses, and psychological syntheses. Obviously, this "reconstruction," in the historical and psychological sense of the term, cannot be an exact copy of the contents of the conscious minds of the actors. We claim to be able to understand all the nuances of love and hate, all the forms of courage and despair, will and feeling, without the expressions on which the image of such affects arises in us, putting us into the same bias in them. But to understand others is still to form in ourselves a distorted, condensed, and muted reproduction of the feelings they experience. If the historian's goal is to recover not only the knowledge produced by historical actors but also their intentions and feelings, such a goal can only be achieved through a kind of mental projection that allows us to experience the desires and feelings of others. Otherwise, understanding a feeling could not depend on having experienced it. A person who has never loved will never understand a person in love, any more than an angry person will understand a phlegmatic person, a coward will understand a hero, or a hero will understand a coward. Likewise, we will understand the gestures, facial expressions, and actions of others more easily if we have often experienced the feelings they express. This understanding is even easier or harder depending on whether our feelings at the time are similar or dissimilar to those of others; in the former case, it will be easier to reproduce the other's feelings in ourselves. In any case, reproducing another person's mental states requires us to be able to reproduce those mental states in ourselves. Such a reproduction is inseparable from the very notion of understanding.

The reconstitution of the mental processes of historical actors is affected by an essential factor, namely, that these thoughts, feelings, and desires, which the observer experiences in a certain way, are not attributed by the observer to himself but to someone else, a non-self. The subjective images that form in the mind of the observer seeking to understand a historical or psychological phenomenon appear in the self as if detached from their roots and attributed to others.

This is a unique complication of the fact that, even in the realm of human experience, the objects of knowledge are never things in themselves but phenomena. The epistemological consequences of this observation have, of course, been denied. History, as has been said, is accessible to us just as nature is, but in a completely different way: The distinction between self and non-self, where both are minds, would have a completely different meaning than in the case of nature, for the two are only numerically, not generically or essentially, different. If no mind can enter into the inner processes of nature, it could at least represent to itself the contents of another mind, which it would be able to reflect completely adequately within itself. On such a fragile pillar, however, no bridge can be built across the gap that separates the self from the non-self. The general equality of nature between the two does not abolish the necessity that all kinds of externalizations, transpositions, and symbolizations mediate between them.

An actual mirroring, an immediate understanding arising from the equality of essence, would be a matter of mind reading and telepathy, or would presuppose a pre-established harmony. On the contrary, the very experience of a mental process is also a process that can only be initiated and ultimately carried out by the subjects themselves.

This perspective only transforms direct parallelism into indirect parallelism. The mental states of one subject can be reproduced in another – with some necessary detours, of course – just as precisely as the words entrusted to one telegraph station are printed out in another, even though the medium that makes this transmission possible is completely heterogeneous with respect to the message transmitted. The much deeper difficulty, however, is that the mental processes I form within myself in this way are not mine. I think of them as historical, which means that I present them not as my ideas but as those of others.

However, if we want to understand other people, it is not enough to reconstruct the mental process they are supposed to follow and say that it is the other person and not me who is experiencing these feelings. Because, according to the presupposition, I must also experience these feelings. And having experienced them, I cannot say that it is the other person and not me. On the contrary, this judgment must immediately accompany these feelings in my consciousness as an afterthought to the original content. This ability to experience feelings that I do not actually experience, and this reconstitution of subjective states that is only possible in subjectivity and yet appears as objective in that very subjectivity, constitute the enigma of historical knowledge. We have hardly begun to solve it with the help of our logical and psychological categories. Undoubtedly, two elements are involved in this knowledge: The production of a mental act and the awareness that this act must be attributed to others. But this way of presenting things separates a posteriori elements that are not perceived as distinct in the process of historical knowledge itself. We are not dealing here with an assembly of parts that have been disassembled, just as our perception of the outside world does not consist of an assembly of sensory information that is distinct from spatial perception. The projection of representations and feelings onto the historical agent is a unitary act. However, this act presupposes that we have experienced the mental processes that we attribute to others. But once the representations are reproduced by the historian and attributed to others, they take on a new form. They become detached from the subjective experience of the historian, just as they become detached from the experience of the historical actor. Their common nature means that both can experience love and hate, both can think and desire, and both can feel pleasure and pain. But assuming that strictly identical feelings can appear in the consciousness of both the observer and the actor, this immediate identity cannot constitute historical knowledge. On the contrary, historical knowledge is the process by which the historian projects reconstructed representations onto the actor.

4.7 The objectification of individual psychic processes

[...]

[The mental processes] must find an understanding analogous to that of rational connections. We understand mental processes when their contents develop logically and follow the necessities arising solely from these contents. This understanding, which is related to content and not to a dynamic law of nature, is based on a singular unity. It is not based on the necessity derived from the natural determinisms of psychical events nor on the necessity derived from logical laws connecting their contents. This understanding implies that what appears in its purely historical factuality as a particular causal sequence of events, often totally irrational, born of blind instincts, without any connection to a meaning and a significance, still has a rationality of its own, even if this is true for a single case. It grasps the unity by which one mental content evolves from another and is linked to another, with the same cohesive force that underlies logical necessity, despite the absence of any logic as such – so certain that the links it establishes may be based on a minimum of given facts! From an epistemological point of view, the link that unites the various features of a historical subject and transforms the complexes of representations accompanying a historical action into a meaningful unity is different from a cause or a reason. It is neither the empirical law of the event nor the formal law of the content, but a third of its own: meaning. Thus, the unity underlying the relationships between observable elements, which depends on their coloring and arrangement, cannot be determined by any law, but can only be experienced empathically. Each element is related to the other according to its content, but only insofar as it refers to an individual unity, in the same way that general conceptual content can be related by logic.

In historical representations, we deduce the psychic elements from each other – not in the manner of syllogism, which proceeds from the universal, but in a synthesis of the imagination. In the domain of the individual par excellence, this synthesis has the power and the right to give the validity of the rational to the contingency of the merely individual fact.

Perhaps this is how the enigma of how we can subjectively represent the state of mind of others is solved. The mediating factor is the particular kind of supra-personal validity that underlies the dynamics and mode of linking elements of a mental image, a validity that has the value of generality without being a conceptual generality.

[...]

4.8 Historical realism

First, we must set aside naive realism, which is limited to applying a theory of knowledge developed for the observable world to internal phenomena. According to realism, truth lies in the correspondence of a thought – correspondence in the sense of a mirror image – with its object, which is considered absolutely external to the observer. In the natural sciences, this concept is considered obsolete. It is sufficient to see that the expression of real events by means of mathematical formulas, atoms, mechanical or dynamic models, only offer a symbolic formulation based on mental constructs. Far from being a copy of the object of knowledge, this symbolic formulation is nothing less than its representation through a system of signs. In the human sciences, however, the sameness of the function of knowledge and its object – since both are mental – still tends to encourage belief in this naturalism, which considers a simple copy of one by the other as possible, and the measure of its fidelity as the measure of the value of knowledge. The historian is often called upon to allow us to see an event "as it really happened". Therefore, it is important to see clearly that all knowledge is the translation of direct experiential data into a new language, a language with its own forms, categories, and rules. By becoming scientific, facts, both internal and external, must answer questions that they never face in reality and cannot answer in their raw form to satisfy the needs of knowledge. Certain specific features have to be emphasized, and subjective relations have to be established on the basis of certain facts, values, or ideas that transcend reality, so to speak. As a result, a new construction is formed from the raw facts – a sui generis construction of a specific type that is subject to its own laws.

4.9 The transformation of reality by the categories of historical inquiry

[...]

The biographical history of a political leader, for example, extracts politically significant events and activities from the continuity of a rich and extensive life. From these events, it reconstructs a political career, which, as such, represents a continuous course of life. However, the moments that the historical construction isolates from this career are not, in reality, disconnected from each other. On the contrary, the behavior of the actor considered in each of these moments depended on internal events from other sources, on the general dispositions of his personality, or on his mood at the time. His behavior at any given moment can only be fully understood by looking at his life as a whole. No historian can capture that whole. So a new whole is constructed from a unifying concept: Politics, which in this generality and abstract clarity may never have entered the subject's consciousness. We should not take too seriously the analogy of the historian who pulls a single thread from the fabric of the actor's life and reconstructs a complete fabric, because this metaphor overemphasizes the continuity in the relationship between the fragments of the historical thread that are woven together. In reality, these fragments are only occasionally and partially connected, and they constitute a "story" for the observer only from the moment the observer decides to make these fragments into a whole.

Again, the difference between psychology and history is evident. Of course, a political decision is a psychological event. But if we want to understand this decision as a psychological event, we have to know all the conditions that were affecting the minds of the actors at the time; we have to take into account the whole life of the actors and take into account many aspects of this life that are alien to politics. Without the joyful and painful moments they experienced, without the ethical and aesthetic emotions they felt, and without the agreements and disagreements that marked their relationships with others, the decision would undoubtedly have been different.

But the political historian does not have to worry about all this because the goal is to construct an unreal being: A being that performs political actions and can be characterized by a perceptible continuity that goes beyond the complexity of psychological sequences that can be ignored. The historian treats his heroes as if they were exclusively political beings, extracting from their actions the political content that only emerged as a reality within all those psychological contexts that have now been neglected. Admittedly, from the moment the historian makes the action understandable in its context and shows, for example, the influence of political constellations, he is thinking psychologically. But we must see that it is a strangely fictitious kind of psychology, an abstract psychology derived from the idea of politics, in which the mental dynamics refer only to the consciousness of the sequence of contents understood according to the logic of the question. These contents are connected according to their immanent laws, instead of each moment emerging separately from the total mental structure of the subject, as in the realistic psychological approach.

The same distinctions can be made when the biographies of scientists are told as the history of the development of their scientific production. Here, only the coherence of their thoughts is in question, insofar as they are oriented towards an objective idea of knowledge. Certainly, these thoughts had to originate as mental processes, but as such, they are coordinated and intertwined with innumerable others, which remain out of consideration here as non-scientific. Thus, it is not the actual lived connections that these biographies offer; the category according to which the connected elements are selected and the connections are established lies beyond their origin as mental realities. It resides in an objective idea placed above them, even though these mental realities constitute the supports that make any synthesis possible and without which there would be no "history".

At this point, we should mention a remarkable mental process that seems to prefigure or illustrate this reconstruction based on an objective concept: The connection of a current content of consciousness with past ones that are objectively related to it. For example, when one has interrupted reading a book and resumes it after days or weeks, what is being read is seamlessly connected to the previous content. The psychological moment carries the continuation given by the meaningful content, as if everything experienced and thought in the meantime did not lie in between. The same is true, of course, of the scientific thoughts of scientists and the political actions of a leader. Our lives are constantly traversed by series that interrupt each other, of which only a relatively small piece unfolds continuously in our consciousness. Meanwhile, each of them, undisturbed and uninfluenced by all the different contents of consciousness that have expired in the meantime, continues its coherent chain according to this meaningful content.

Thus, it appears that the psyche spontaneously performs a structuring operation on the contents of consciousness, and this operation obeys strictly logical criteria. It is this process of historical selection and structuring that determines the psychological reality that is experienced. This function, by which the psyche restores the logical continuity of interrupted sequences, perhaps explains not only the possibility but also the attraction of history, in which the historical actor is defined by a role and a well-defined influence on the course of events. We could even go so far as to speak of a common substrate of reality and history.

However, there remains a fundamental difference in meaning between the two. From a purely external point of view, we can describe the course of life, with the inevitable symbolism that it implies, by the fact that consciousness selects certain fragments from the innumerable series of events that affect us in order to constitute itself through them. We have just seen that the mind has the peculiar ability to ignore interruptions and to correct, to some extent, the apparent inconsistencies of things and ideas. But beyond this outer picture lies a deeper inner duality: The subjectively lived life has its starting point, its accents, and its meaning in the self, that is, in the dynamics and productivity of the mind. From this point of view, the inner reality is perceived as a comprehensible and continuous whole that is lived from the variable, heterogeneous, fragmentary pieces of these series.

Despite the fact that the psyche has the ability to go back and find the abandoned thread, which allows it to restore continuity between disparate states of consciousness, reality takes on a completely different outlook depending on whether it is perceived from the point of view of the self or from that of the meaning of objective contents. But it is from the latter that historical observation takes its point of departure, for it is from them that it selects from the whole of reality and gathers and articulates the parts.

[...]

Notes

1   Simmel, G. (first ed. 1892/ second ed. 1905/ third ed. 1907/ 1923). *Die Probleme der Geschichtsphilosophie: Eine erkenntnistheoretische Studie* [Problems in the Philosophy of Pistory: An Epistemological Study]. Foreword to the third edition (pp. v–vii), Chap. 1 (p. 1; pp. 4–26; pp. 35–42; pp. 50–51; pp. 52–53; pp. 59–63). Leipzig: Verlag von Duncker& Humblot.

2   Translator's note: See Knapp (1891).

3   To explain these phenomena, it is interesting to consider a characteristic feature of the structure of knowledge. Knowledge is based on the assumption that a constellation of causes will always produce the same effect. If the repetition of the same constellation seems to produce a different result, we conclude that this constellation is not really the same as the previous one, and that the differences between them have escaped us. This is why we can grasp and identify the purely individual psychological elements only very imperfectly, if at all: their nuances, their intensity, and their interactions largely escape us. General concepts such as love and hate, feelings of power or depression, intelligence and will, selfishness and self-denial, and many others, are used to describe, in a very approximate way, highly diverse phenomena. We become more aware of this diversity as the effects of such a constellation unfold.

A very simple example is the fact that the same mental energy, depending on its intensity, can produce completely different, even contradictory, effects. For example, we know that love can be extinguished by separation from its object, but in other cases, this separation can also result in fervent passion. The reason for this difference is undoubtedly that the mental energy involved is weaker in the first case than in the second. Depending on the intensity of the passion, there must be a threshold above which the psychological effect of separation from the beloved object is reversed. The same is true of sensations: There are thresholds beyond which pleasure turns into pain. These reversals correspond to purely quantitative variations in stimulation. As far as emotions are concerned, we lack the appropriate measuring instruments or concepts to express these kinds of effects, even approximately. We have to make do with general concepts that are insensitive to these variations in intensity, so that we use the same names to refer to very different realities and causes, and we get the impression that the same causes can produce different effects. However, this imperfection may not be without a deeper basis; let us note that it concerns not only our inability to express quantitative differences, but also our inability to express individual accents, tones, and fluctuations. Perhaps it implies that the purely individual aspects of a mental process cannot be expressed scientifically or conceptually, and therefore cannot be accessed by knowledge as such. We may be able to provide a scientifically comprehensible reconstruction of the mental state only insofar as there is something generally human (at least relatively) in it, something common to both the knowing subject and the object of knowledge.

Of course, this commonality is neither the cause nor a guarantee that this knowledge is correct; it is only a condition of knowledge. The fact that knowledge requires the use of universal concepts that ignore individual diversity thus sets its limits, but these can be seen as defining and formally expressing its nature and its possibilities.

4   One of the epistemological roots of historicism is the lack of clarity about the presuppositions of historical constructs that transcend any particular historical process. This clarification is especially necessary and urgent when the historical facts under consideration are not only mental in nature — all historical facts are ultimately mental — but also have mental content. This is especially true of the history of science, religion, or art. To understand the development of science or art at a particular time and place is to understand the content of scientific and artistic works and their relations to each other, independent of the particular time and place in which they appeared. It has been argued that in order to understand Kant, it is necessary to deduce him historically. But if it were impossible to grasp the content of the pre-Kantian doctrines and their relation to Kant's work from a logical and psychological point of view, if this relation did not constitute a series that could be understood independently of its historical realization, then the historical succession between the earlier philosophers and Kant would correspond to the discontinuity of mere moments in time, and the "historical deduction" of Kant's work would actually consist only in placing it in its historical context. Conversely, we can argue that the "historical deduction" of Kant first implies an objective understanding of Kant and the other philosophers, not only of the individual doctrines, but of the objective relationship, independent of any consideration of "date," between their contents.

The same is true of art history. It shows us how the depiction of movement and relief has evolved, how the concept of juxtaposition and perspective has changed, how the meaning of color and form has shifted, and it illustrates these developments through specific artists. But the succession of these artistic personalities would never have the continuous coherence of a unified historical series if their achievements did not give instructions to each other according to their factual content and without any consideration of their historical placement, if they did not form an ideal series, comparable — cum grano salis — to the series of upper clause, lower clause, and last clause in a syllogism. Of course, psychologically, the elements of this series also constitute a temporal sequence, but they would have no unity if there were not a timeless connection of meaning between them, indifferent to all that precedes and follows.

The rigidity of the Byzantine and Gothic groups was followed by the individualizing disorder of the Quattrocento, then unified in the regular harmonies of the early Renaissance, which from the end of the Cinquecento began to collapse, become hollow formalism, or degenerated into wild confusion. But in order for these different moments to constitute a "historical" sequence of real, temporally related phenomena, we must be able to understand them in terms of their intrinsic meaning and to grasp their internal relationships from the point of view of artistic logic. Otherwise, they would simply amount to an incoherent succession of elements devoid of relationships, a succession that lacks the principle and the possibility of grouping into series, that is, the condition under which it is possible to identify this series within the infinite variety of events.

Historicism, because of its empiricist orientation, believes that it can derive this unity from "historical reality" itself. On the contrary, we must perceive this unity in order for reality to appear historical to us at all.

References

Knapp, G. F. (1891). Die Landarbeiter. In *Knechtschaft und Freiheit. Gesammelte Vorträge [The agricultural workers. In bondage and freedom. Collected lectures].* Leipzig: Duncker & Humblot.

von Sybel, L. (1857). *Geschichte der Revolutionszeit von 1789 bis 1800 [History of the revolutionary period from 1789 to 1800].* Heidelberg: J.C.B. Mohr.

5   Max Weber (1922)

The basic concepts of sociology[1]

Prefatory remark

The method of this introduction, which cannot be dispensed with, but is inevitably abstract and detached from reality, does not pretend to be novel in any way. On the contrary, it has no other ambition than to formulate in a more suitable and slightly more accurate way (which may certainly make it seem pedantic) what all empirical sociology really means when it talks about the same things. This holds true even when apparently unusual or new expressions are used. Compared to the author's article published in *Logos* (IV, 1913, p. 253 ff.)[2], the terminology is simplified as much as possible and thus modified in several places in order to be most easily understood. The need for the highest possible conceptual sharpness cannot always be reconciled with a form easily popularized and it must, if necessary, forego the latter.

On the concept of "understanding [Verstehen]," refer to K. Jaspers' *Allgemeine Psychopathologie* [General Psychopathology][3] (some of Rickert's remarks in the second edition of *Grenzen der natur wissenschaftlichen Begriffsbildung* [Limits to the formation of concepts in the natural sciences][4] and in particular Simmel's discussions in *Problemen der Geschichtsphilosophie* [Problems of the Philosophy of History][5] are also relevant here). From a methodological point of view, I refer again, as I have done on several occasions, to the approach of F. Gottl in his book, which is admittedly difficult to understand and whose ideas are not always fully elaborated: *Die Herrschaft des Wortes* [The Rule of the Word][6]. Regarding the subject matter, I refer primarily to F. Tönnies' fine work *Gemeinschaft und Gesellschaft* [Community and Society][7], as well as to the highly misleading book of R. Stammler, *Wirtschaft und Recht nach der materialistischen Geschichtsauffassung* [Economy and Law according to the Materialist Conception of History][8], and to my critique of it in *Archiv f. Sozialwissensch* XXIV (1907)[9], which already contains a large part of the foundations of what follows. I depart from Simmel's method in *Soziologie* [Sociology][10] and in *Philos. des Geldes* [Philosophy of Money][11] by distinguishing as far as possible between the subjectively *intended* and the objectively *valid* "meaning," two meanings which Simmel not only does not always distinguish but often deliberately conflates.

DOI: 10.4324/9781032627021-5

§ 1 Sociology (in the sense given here to this very ambiguous word) is a science that aims to understand social action interpretively and thus to explain its course and effects causally. Human behavior (whether overt or covert, omission or forbearance) is called "action," if and insofar as the acting individual or individuals attach a subjective meaning to it. But an action is said to be "social" if, according to its intended meaning, it refers to the behavior of others and is oriented toward it in its course.

5.1 Methodological foundations

1) "Meaning" here is either (a) the actual intended meaning in the given concrete case of a particular actor or the average and approximate intended meaning attributable to a given plurality of actors, or (b) the subjectively intended meaning according to a conceptually constructed pure type and attributed to the actor or actors conceived as types. In no case does it refer to an objectively "correct" or metaphysically "true" meaning. Therein lies the difference between the empirical sciences of action, such as sociology and history, and all dogmatic disciplines, such as jurisprudence, logic, ethics, and aesthetics, which seek the "true" and "valid" meaning of their objects.

2) The line between meaningful action and merely reactive behavior (as identified here), to which no subjective meaning is ascribed, is quite fluid. A substantial part of all behavior relevant to sociology, especially purely traditional action (see below), lies in between. In some instances of psychophysical processes, there is no meaningful, that is, understandable, action; in other cases, it exists only for the specialist; many mystical experiences that cannot be adequately articulated in words are not fully understandable to one who does not have access to such experiences. Conversely, the ability to perform an action similar to that of another is not a condition of understanding: "One does not need to be Caesar to understand Caesar." The full potential to relive an experience is significant for the evidence of understanding, but not an absolute precondition for the interpretation of meaning. Understandable and non-understandable components of a process are often intertwined and bound up together.

3) All interpretation, like all "science" in general, strives for "evidence." Evidence of understanding can be either rational (and then either logical or mathematical) or empathic (emotional, or artistically receptive in nature). In the realm of action, what is rationally evident is primarily what is intellectually understood in its intended context of meaning [sinnzusammenhang] in a complete and transparent way; what is empathically evident is what is fully relived in its experiential context. The highest degree of rational understanding, that is, a clear and direct intellectual grasp, applies especially to the relations of meaning between mathematical or logical propositions. We understand meaningfully and completely unambiguously what someone means when using the proposition 2x2=4 or the Pythagorean theorem in reasoning or argumentation,

or when carrying a logical line of reasoning consistent with our ingrained modes of thinking. In the same way, we understand the meaning of the action of a person who, in order to achieve certain given ends, chooses the appropriate means from the facts of experience that are "known" to us, and draws the consequences that clearly follow from them (according to our experience). The interpretation of such rationally oriented action towards an end – for the understanding of the choice of means – has the highest degree of evidence. With a lower, but sufficient, degree of certainty for our need for explanation, we also understand those "errors" (including "problem entanglements") that we ourselves are prone to make or whose source we can perceive through empathy.

On the other hand, we often struggle to fully understand certain ultimate "ends" and "values" that, according to experience, can guide human action; even if we can grasp them intellectually, we find it all the more difficult to make them understandable through empathetic imagination the more radically they depart from our own ultimate values. Depending on the situation, we may have to settle for a purely intellectual understanding of such values, or, failing that, we must simply accept them as given. We can then make sense of the course of action motivated by these values, as far as possible, on the basis of clues interpreted intellectually or roughly experienced through empathy. This includes, for example, many cases of religious and charitable zeal for people who are not sensitive to them. The same applies to rationalistic radicalisms (e.g., the fanatical defense of "human rights") for those who, for their part, abhor these orientations. The more we ourselves are sensitive to actual affects such as fear, anger, ambition, envy, jealousy, love, enthusiasm, pride, thirst for revenge, piety, devotion, desires of all kinds, and to the irrational reactions resulting from them (seen from the point of view of purposeful rational action), the more we are able to experience them emotionally, or in any case, even when their intensity absolutely exceeds our own possibilities, to understand them meaningfully with empathy and to take into account their influence on the course and means of action.

For the scientific purpose of constructing types, all components of personal behavior conditioned by affect, which influence action, are investigated and most clearly represented as "deviations" from a conceptually pure type of purposeful rational course of action. For example, to explain a "stock market panic," it is appropriate first to determine how the action would have unfolded without the influence of irrational effects, and then to introduce these irrational components as "disturbances." Similarly, in the case of a political or military action, it is appropriate to first determine how the action would have proceeded, given the adequate knowledge of all the circumstances and intentions of the actors involved, and assuming the choice of means to be strictly rational and based on the recognized rules of experience. Only in this way can such deviations be causally attributed to irrational factors. In such cases, the construction of a strictly purposive-rational action serves sociology because of its immediate intelligibility and its univocity, which adheres to rationality as an 'ideal-type' model. In contrast, the influence of various types of irrationalities (affects, errors) can be understood as "deviations" from the course of action expected in the case of purely rational behavior. In this respect, and only for reasons of methodological expediency, the method of the "understanding" sociology is "rationalistic." This method is obviously not to be understood as implying a rationalist bias of sociology, but only as a methodological device. It does not, therefore, imply a belief in the effective dominance of the rational over human life, for there is no question, to say the least, of the extent to which rational considerations do or do not determine actual action in reality. But one cannot deny the obvious danger of inappropriate rationalistic interpretations, as experience unfortunately continues to confirm.

4) In all the sciences of action, meaningless processes and objects come into consideration as: Cause, result, stimulation, or inhibition of human action.

But "meaningless" does not mean "inanimate" or "non-human." Any process or state without meaningful content, whether animate or inanimate, human or nonhuman, remains meaningless insofar as it cannot be related to the "means" and "end" of action, but only plays the role of cause, stimulation, or inhibition. Conversely, any artifact, such as a "machine," can only be interpreted and understood in terms of the meaning that human action (whose aims can be very diverse) has given (or wanted to give) to its production and use; without recourse to this meaning, it remains totally incomprehensible. What is understandable about it, therefore, is the reference of human action to this meaning, either as a "means" or as an "end," which the actor(s) had in mind and towards which their action was directed. It is only in this respect that an understanding of such objects arises. The flooding of the Dollard in 1277 has (perhaps!) a "historical" significance as the trigger of certain population migrations of considerable historical magnitude. Human mortality and the whole organic cycle of life, from the vulnerability of a child to that of an elderly person are, of course, of enormous sociological importance because of the many ways in which human action has been and continues to be influenced by this condition. To another category of phenomena belong incomprehensible statements about the experience of psychological or psychophysiological states such as fatigue, habituation, memory, etc., but also, for example, some typical states of euphoria under certain conditions of ascetic mortification, or typical variations of certain reactions, according to their rhythm, type, singularity, etc. In the end, however, the situation is the same as in the case of other incomprehensible data: Just as the person acting in practice accepts them as "data" to be recknoned with, so does the understanding observer.

It is possible that future research will also discover uninterpretable regularities in certain meaningful behaviors, as little as has been the case so far. Differences in biological-genetic endowments (of "races"), for example, would be accepted by sociology as data, on a par with physiological facts such as nutritional requirements or the effects of aging on action, if and to the extent that conclusive statistical evidence of their influence on sociologically relevant types of behavior were provided. Acknowledging their causal significance would not change in the least the task of sociology (and the action sciences in general), which is to understand meaning-oriented action through interpretation. It would merely introduce, at certain points within the comprehensibly interpretable motivational contexts, non-meaningful facts of the same order as others already mentioned above (e.g., typical relationships between the frequency of certain types of action orientation or the degree of typical rationality and the cranial index, or skin color, or whatever other hereditary physiological quality).

5) Understanding can firstly mean the direct comprehension of the meaning of an action, including a verbal utterance. For instance, we truly "understand" the meaning of the sentence $2\times2=4$ that we hear or read (direct rational understanding of ideas), or an outburst of anger manifested in facial expressions, interjections, irrational movements (direct understanding of irrational affects), or the behavior of a lumberjack or of someone who grabs a door handle to close it or who points a gun at an animal (direct understanding of rational actions). However, understanding may also mean, secondly, explanatory understanding [erklärendes Verstehen]. We "understand" in terms of motive the meaning that the person who said or wrote the sentence $2\times2=4$ gave it at that moment and in that context, when performing an accounting calculation, a scientific demonstration, a technical computation, or some other action, so that according to our interpretation of the context to which this sentence "belongs," it acquires an intelligible meaning (rational understanding of motivation). We understand the act of chopping wood or aiming a gun not only on a direct level but also on a motivational level. This is true when we know that the woodcutter did it to earn a living, for personal use or recreation (rational motive), or because he "let off steam" (irrational motive). Similarly, when the person who fired the gun acted on orders with the aim of executing or combating enemies (rational motive) or out of revenge (affective motive, so in this sense, irrational). Finally, we understand anger on the level of motivation if we know that it is driven by jealousy, hurt vanity, or scorned honor (affectively conditioned, therefore irrational motives). In all these cases, which involve comprehensible relations of meaning, understanding is considered as explaining the actual course of action. Thus, for a science concerned with the meaning of action, "explaining" is akin to "understanding": It involves grasping the complex of meanings [Sinnzusammenhangs] within which a subjectively comprehensible action is embedded. On the causal significance of this "explanation," see no. 6 below.

In all these cases, even in the case of affective processes, we want to refer to the subjective meaning of the event, including the context of meaning, as the "intended" meaning (thereby going beyond the usual language usage, which tends to speak of "intending" in this sense only for rational and purposive action).

6) In all these cases, "understanding" refers to the interpretive comprehension of a) what is really intended in the individual case (e.g., in historical observation); b) what is intended on average and approximately (e.g., in sociological observation of collective phenomena); or c) what is scientifically constructed for the pure (ideal) type of a common phenomenon. The concepts and "laws" posited by the pure economic theory offer an example of such ideal-typical constructions. They depict how a particular human action would proceed if it were purely rational, unaffected by errors or emotions, and if it were further explicitly oriented towards a single (economic) objective. In reality, actions follow this course only in rare instances (e.g., the stock market), and even then, they only approximate the ideal type (for the purpose of such constructions, see *Archiv für Sozialwissenschaft*, xix, p. 64 ff. and below, no. 8).

Every interpretation strives for evidence. But an interpretation, however evidential it may be from the point of view of meaning, cannot, on this account, claim to be also the causally valid interpretation. It remains a plausible causal hypothesis. First, pretended "motives" and "repressions" (i.e., initially unacknowledged motives) often enough conceal the real context of the orientation of one's action from the person acting in such a way that even subjectively sincere self-reports have only relative value. In such cases, it is up to the sociologist to determine and interpret this meaning, even though it was not, or mostly not, fully consciously "intended" in concrete terms (this is a borderline case of interpretation of meaning).

Second, certain external features of an action that we consider to be "identical" or "similar" may stem from very different contexts of meaning in the person or persons acting. Similarly, although situations appear "similar" to us, we "understand" very different, often almost contradictory actions in terms of meaning (Simmel provides examples in his work *Problems of the Philosophy of History*).

Third, persons acting in given situations often experience conflicting, competing drives, all of which we "understand." Experience shows, however, that in many cases it is impossible to estimate, even roughly and in any case without certainty, the relative strength with which the various meanings underlying the "struggle of motives," meanings that are equally comprehensible to us, are expressed in action. The actual outcome of the struggle of motives alone can provide insight into this.

As with any hypothesis, the understandable interpretation of meaning can only be verified by comparison with the actual course of action. This can be done with relative precision in the unfortunately rare and specific cases that lend themselves to psychological experimentation, and with varying degrees of approximation in the limited cases of statistically described and unambiguously interpreted collective phenomena. For the rest, there remains only the possibility of comparing the largest possible number of historical or everyday events that, although similar in nature, differ on the crucial point of the "motive" or "cause" under investigation; this is an important task of comparative sociology. Often, however, the only option left is the uncertain method of "thought experiments," which involves searching for the components of the motive chain and reconstructing the probable course of events in order to arrive at a causal imputation.

For example, the so-called "Gresham's law" in economics is a rationally unambiguous interpretation of human action under given conditions and under the ideal-typical condition of purely purposeful rational action. Only the experience, ideally expressed in a "statistical" way, of the actual disappearance of undervalued coins from circulation can tell us to what extent one actually acts in accordance with this law. In this case, our information confirms its broad validity. In reality, the empirical facts preceded the interpretation, but without this successful interpretation, our need for causal understanding would obviously remain unsatisfied. Conversely, without evidence that an individual's behavior actually occurs to some extent, as we assume, such a "law," however apparently accurate, would be a worthless construct for understanding actual action. In this example, the correspondence between the theoretical interpretation of meaning and its empirical verification is quite conclusive, and there are enough cases for the verification to be considered established.

Eduard Meyer's ingenious hypothesis about the causal role played by the battles of Marathon, Salamis, and Plataea in the development of the peculiarities of the Hellenic (and thus Western) culture implies a meaningful interpretation of certain symptomatic facts having to do with the attitude of Greek oracles and prophets toward the Persians. It can only be confirmed by the evidence drawn from the example of Persian behavior in cases where they were victorious (as in Jerusalem, Egypt, and Asia Minor), and this evidence will necessarily remain imperfect in many respects. There must be significant rational evidence to support the hypothesis. However, in many cases where the causal imputation in historical interpretation seems obvious, the possibility of conducting such a test, as was possible in the previous case, is lacking, and the imputation ultimately remains a "hypothesis."

7) By "motive," we refer to a complex of subjective meanings that appears to the actor himself or to an observer as a meaningful "reason" for behavior. The interpretation of a coherent behavior can be considered "meaningfully adequate" as long as, according to our usual ways of thinking and feeling, the relation of its constituent elements appears to us as a typical relation of meaning (we use to say "correct"). Conversely, the interpretation of a sequence of events will be termed "causally adequate" when, according to the rules of experience, this sequence is likely to always recur in the same manner.

An example of adequacy from the point of view of meaning is the solution of an arithmetic problem according to our usual norms of calculation or thought. Statistically speaking, a causally adequate interpretation of the same phenomenon would satisfy the probability that, according to established rules of experience, a typically correct or incorrect solution would actually occur. Therefore, causal explanation means the assertion that, according to an estimable probability rule, and in the ideally quantifiable, rare case, a certain observed (internal or external) event is followed by (or coincides with) a certain other event.

A true causal interpretation of a given action means that its external execution and its motive are correctly recognized and, at the same time, meaningfully understandable in its context. A true causal interpretation of a typical action (understandable type of action) means that the course of events claimed to be typical appears to some extent meaningfully adequate and can be determined to some extent as causally adequate.

If meaning adequacy is lacking, then regardless of the degree of quantifiable regularity of the course of events (both external and mental), the statistical probability is not understandable (or only imperfectly so). Conversely, for the domain of sociological knowledge, even the most obvious adequacy at the level of meaning is causally correct only if there is evidence of some chance that the action actually tends to follow the course considered meaningful.

Only those statistical regularities that correspond to a comprehensible intended meaning of social action are understandable types of action (in the literal sense used here), that is, "sociological rules." Conversely, such rational constructions of a meaningfully understandable action can only be considered as sociological types of real events if they can be observed in reality, at least approximately. But the actual likelihood of a given course of action occurring does not necessarily increase in parallel with the corresponding sequence of understandable meanings. Whether this is the case, however, can only be demonstrated in each case by actual experience.

Statistics exist for phenomena devoid of subjective meaning (death rates, fatigue phenomena, machine performance, precipitation rates) in exactly the same way as for meaningful phenomena. However, we only speak of sociological statistics (such as those relating to crimes, occupations, prices, and crops) when the phenomena are meaningful. Naturally, there are many cases where both types are involved, as in crop yield statistics.

8) Processes and regularities, that we do not qualify here as sociological facts or rules because they are devoid of subjective meaning are no less important. This is true even for sociology as we understand it here, which is limited to the understanding sociology, which cannot and should not be imposed on anyone. For crucial methodological reasons, these processes and regularities are considered at a distinct level from understandable action, specifically as the 'conditions', 'causes', 'inhibitions', and 'stimulation' of the latter.

9) Action, in the sense of a meaningful, understandable orientation of behavior, exists for us only as the behavior of one or more individual persons. For other purposes of knowledge, it may be useful or necessary to conceive of the individual as an association of "cells" or a complex of biochemical reactions, or to consider the "psychic" life of that individual as consisting of individual units (however these may be defined). This undoubtedly allows us to gain valuable knowledge in the form of causal relationships. Nevertheless, we

cannot subjectively understand the behavior of these elements expressed in terms of rules. The same is true of psychic elements, which we understand all the less the more precisely they are described by the procedures of the natural sciences: This is never the way of interpretation in terms of intended meaning. For sociology (in the literal sense used here, as well as for history), however, it is precisely the meaning of the context of action that is to be understood. We can, at least in principle, observe or try to understand the behavior of physiological units such as cells or any psychic element. From this, we derive rules ("laws"), and with the help of these, we can causally "explain" individual processes, that is, subsume them under rules. The interpretation of action, however, takes these facts and rules into account to the same extent as it takes other meaningless facts into account (e.g., physical, astronomical, geological, meteorological, geographical, botanical, zoological, physiological, and anatomical, psychopathological facts that are unrelated to subjective meaning, or the natural conditions of technical facts).

For other purposes of knowledge (e.g., law) or for practical purposes, it may be appropriate and even necessary to treat social structures such as "states," "cooperatives," "public companies," and "foundations" in the same way as individuals, for example, as subjects of rights and duties or as perpetrators of legally relevant acts. For the understanding interpretation of action, however, these structures are merely processes and contexts of specific actions by individuals, since only these individuals can act with comprehensible, meaning-oriented intentions. Nevertheless, sociology cannot ignore these forms of collective thought derived from other modes of observation, even for its own purposes. In fact, the interpretation of action relates to these collective concepts in three ways:

a) Language itself often requires the use of similar collective concepts (often designated in the same way) in order to create an intelligible terminology. For example, both legal language and everyday language use the term 'state' to refer to both the legal concept and the facts of social action to which the legal rules apply. For sociology, the 'state' does by no means consist only, or necessarily, of legally relevant elements. In any case, for sociology, there is no such thing as an 'acting' collective personality. When it speaks of 'state' or 'nation' or 'corporation' or 'family' or 'army corps' or similar 'entities', it merely refers to a particular course of actual or possible social action by individuals, and thus imposes a completely different meaning on the legal term, which it uses for its precision and familiarity.

b) The interpretation of action must take into account the fundamental fact that collective concepts, which are an integral part of everyday or legal (or other specialized) thinking, represent ideas about something that partly exists in reality and partly has normative authority in the minds of real people (not only judges and officials, but also the "public"), who orient their actions according to these ideas. To this extent, these ideas have a powerful, often dominant, causal significance for the course of action of real people, primarily in relation to what must be or, conversely, what must not be. In this way, the modern "state" exists largely as a complex of specific joint actions of individuals. It exists because some people base their actions on the idea that it exists or ought to exist, and thus that orders of a juridical nature are valid. We shall return to this point later. Although it would be extremely pedantic and cumbersome, it would be technically possible for sociology to completely eliminate these common language terms, which designate not only legal concepts but also real events, and replace them with entirely new words, at least for this important matter. Even this would be out of the question.

c) The method of so-called "organicist" sociology, classically exemplified by Schäffle's (1881) work "Bau und Leben des sozialen Körpers" [Construction and Life of the Social Body], attempts to explain social interaction starting from the "whole" (e.g., a 'national economy'). Within this whole, the individuals and their behavior are then interpreted in the same way as physiology treats the function of a bodily "organ" within the "household economy" of the organism, that is, from the point of view of the "maintenance" of the whole. Hence the famous statement from a physiologist in one of his lectures: "Section x: The Spleen. Of the spleen, gentlemen, we know nothing. So much for the spleen!" In fact, the lecturer indeed "knew" a lot about the spleen: Its position, size, shape, etc., but he could not specify its "function," and he called this inability "ignorance." We will not discuss here whether this kind of functional approach to the "parts" of a "whole" should necessarily be considered as definitive in other disciplines. We know that biochemical and biomechanical approaches cannot, in principle, be satisfied with this. For an interpretive sociology, functional language may be useful for two reasons: 1) To serve as a practical illustration and provisional orientation of research (in which case it can be extremely useful and necessary, but also extremely detrimental if its cognitive value is overestimated and its concepts illegitimately reified); 2) To help us, under certain circumstances, to discover social actions whose interpretive understanding is important for explaining a context. But this is where the work of sociology, as understood here, begins. In the case of "social structures" (as opposed to "organisms"), we are able to go beyond the mere determination of functional relationships and rules ("laws") and provide something that is forever inaccessible to the "natural sciences" (in the sense that they establish causal laws for events and structures and "explain" individual events on the basis of them): Namely an "understanding" of the behavior of the individuals involved, whereas we can only functionally grasp the behavior of cells and then determine it according to the rules of its course. This additional achievement of interpretive explanation over observational explanation comes at a price – the more hypothetical and fragmented character of its results. But this is precisely what distinguishes sociological knowledge.

The extent to which animal behavior is "understandable" to us, and vice versa – both cases raise highly problematic questions about the meaning and scope of this understanding – and the extent to which a sociology of human relationships with animals, whether with domestic or wild animals, could theoretically exist are questions we will not address here. Many animals "understand" commands, anger, love, hostility, and clearly respond to them, not only mechanically and instinctively, but also appear to do so in a conscious way, oriented by meaning and experience. Our capacity for empathy is certainly not much better when it comes to the behavior of "primitive peoples." Either we have no reliable means of identifying subjective facts in animals, or what we have is at best highly inadequate. The problems of animal psychology are as fascinating as they are thorny. In particular, the social associations observed among animals are of the most diverse kinds, ranging from monogamous and polygamous "families" to herds, packs, and finally "states" with a functional division of labor. The degree of functional differentiation in these animal societies does not necessarily correlate with the degree of organic or morphological differentiation of the species. For example, termites show a higher degree of functional differentiation, and consequently, their artifacts are more differentiated than those of ants and bees. In this field, it is generally accepted that the purely functional approach, which focuses on determining the roles of different types of individuals ("kings," "queens," "workers," "soldiers," "drones," "propagators," "surrogate queens," etc.) that are crucial for species preservation (i.e., feeding, defense, reproduction, and regeneration of the animal societies concerned), is often the definitive stage of research, at least for the time being. What has gone beyond this has long been pure speculation, or studies of the extent to which heredity on the one hand and the environment on the other might be involved in the development of these "social dispositions." This marked the debate between Götte and Weismann. The latter's theory of the "omnipotence of natural selection" has no empirical basis. Serious research, of course, agrees that the above limitation to functional knowledge is a necessary compromise, but hopefully only a temporary one. For more information on the state of termite research, see, for example, Escherich (1909).

It is quite easy to see the importance of the roles of the various differentiated types for the "preservation of the species," and how this differentiation can be explained without assuming the heredity of acquired characteristics, or conversely, if this assumption is made (and then specifying how it is interpreted). However, we also want to understand: 1. What determines the initial differentiation of the still neutral and undifferentiated species type, and 2. What causes the differentiated individual to behave (on average) in ways that effectively serve the conservation interests of the differentiated group. Wherever research has made progress in this regard, it has been through experimental evidence (or conjecture) concerning the role of chemical stimuli or physiological facts in the case of the individual organism (such as nutritional processes, parasitic castration, etc.). To what extent there is any hope of proving experimentally the existence of a "psychological" and "meaningful" orientation in these matters, even the expert could hardly say. The idea of a verifiable concept of the psyche of these social animals, based on meaningful "understanding," seems to be an ideal goal only within narrow limits. In any case, the "understanding" of human social action is not to be expected from it, but rather the opposite, since in animal psychology, human analogies are and must be used. We can perhaps expect these analogies to be useful in answering the question of how, in the early stages of human social differentiation, the relationship between purely mechanical and instinctive differentiating factors and comprehensible individual actions, especially those pursued rationally and consciously, is to be assessed. Understanding sociology must, of course, recognize that even in the early stages of human development, the former component is quite predominant, and it should recognize its continuing influence in later stages, sometimes in a decisive way. All "traditional" actions (§ 2) and large areas of "charisma" (Chapter III) as seeds of forms of psychological "contagion" and thus the carrier of sociological "developmental stimuli," are very close to such processes, with imperceptible transitions that are only biologically understandable and cannot be explained in terms of subjective motives, or only in fragments. All this, however, does not relieve sociology of the task of doing what it alone can do, even if it is aware of the narrow limits within which it is confined.

The various works of Othmar Spann – often rich in good ideas alongside occasional misunderstandings and, above all, arguments based on pure value judgments that do not belong to empirical investigation – are therefore undoubtedly right in emphasizing the importance of preliminary functional questioning for any sociology (what he calls the "universalistic method") – a point that no one seriously disputes. We certainly must first know what kind of action is functionally important for survival (but also and especially for cultural type!) and for the further development of a certain orientation of social action before it becomes possible to investigate how it came about and what motives drive it. First of all, it is necessary to know what a "king," a "civil servant," an "entrepreneur," a "pimp," a "magician" does, that is, what kind of typical "action" (which justifies the classification of an individual in one of these categories) is significant and relevant for the analysis, before one can proceed to this analysis itself (this is what H. Rickert means by "value relatedness").

But it is only through this analysis that we can achieve what the sociological understanding of the actions of typically differentiated human beings (and only among human beings) can and therefore should accomplish. The tremendous misunderstanding of the confusion between the "individualist" method and individualistic valuation (in any possible sense) must be eliminated, as well as the view that the inevitable (but relatively) rational character of concept formation means a belief in the predominance of rational motives or even a positive evaluation of "rationalism." Even a socialist economy should also be understood sociologically by an "individualist" method, that is, based on the actions of individuals – the types of "officials" found there – just as exchange transactions, for example, should be interpreted by the theory of marginal utility (or a "better" method, if one is found, but similar in this respect). Here too, the decisive empirical and sociological work begins only with the question of the motives that led and continue to lead the various officials and members of this "community" to behave in such a way that it came into being and continues to exist. Any functional conceptualization (starting from the "whole") serves only as a preparatory work for this kind of investigation, the usefulness and necessity of which, if properly carried out, are, of course, undeniable.

10) It is usual to call certain theories of the understanding sociology "laws" – for example, Gresham's "law" – "laws" that represent typical chances, substantiated by observation, indicating that a certain course of social action is to be expected under certain conditions, which are understandable in terms of typical motives and of typical meanings intended by the actors. This understanding is the clearest when purely rational motives underlie the typically observed course of action (or are assumed as the basis of the methodically constructed type for reasons of convenience), and when the relationship between means and ends is unambiguous according to the principles of experience (where, for example, the means are "unavoidable"). In such cases, it is permissible to affirm that, as long as the action is strictly rational, it cannot deviate from its course because, given their clearly defined ends, the actors have only these means at their disposal and no others for "technical" reasons. This very case shows how wrong it is to consider any kind of "psychology" as the ultimate "basis" of understanding sociology. Today, everyone understands "psychology" in different ways. Specific methodological objectives justify a separation of the "physical" and the "psychic" for the scientific treatment of certain processes, which in this sense is alien to the disciplines of action. The results of psychological research, which in reality studies the "psychic" only with the means of the natural sciences, and therefore does not interpret human behavior, - which is quite different - through its subjective meaning, whatever the nature of its method, can naturally become important for sociological research in certain cases, as for any other science. In general, however, sociology has no closer relationship with this kind of psychology than with any other discipline. The source of the error lies in the notion of "psychic": What is not "physical" would be "psychic." But the meaning of an arithmetical conclusion that someone is thinking about is not "psychic." A person's rational consideration of whether or not a certain action is beneficial to a particular interest, given the expected consequences and the decision made on the basis of the result of this assessment, is hardly made more understandable to us by taking into account "psychological" considerations. Yet it is on such rational premises that sociology (including economics) bases most of its "laws." On

the other hand, it is clear that the kind of psychology which uses the method of subjective understanding can make important and decisive contributions to the sociological explanation of the irrationalities of action. But this does not change the basic methodological situation.

11) Sociology, as has already been assumed on several occasions, forms concepts of types and seeks general rules of events. This distinguishes it from history, which seeks causal analysis and explanation of individual, culturally significant actions, structures, and personalities. Conceptualization in sociology draws its material to a large extent, but not exclusively, from the realities of action that are also relevant from the point of view of history. It forms its concepts and seeks its rules, particularly from the perspective of its contribution to the causal explanation of historically and culturally important phenomena. As with any generalizing science, its abstractions must be relatively devoid of concrete meaning in relation to historical reality. What it must offer in compensation is greater univocity of its concepts. This greater univocity requires the highest possible degree of adequacy of meaning, such as is sought in the formation of sociological concepts. As we have seen so far, this goal can be most fully achieved in the case of concepts and generalizations applied to rational action (in relation to values or to given ends). However, sociology also seeks to grasp irrational phenomena (mystical, prophetic, spiritual, and affective) using theoretical concepts that are adequate in terms of meaning. In all cases, whether rational or irrational, it abstracts itself from reality and serves to know it by indicating the extent to which a concrete historical phenomenon can be subsumed under one or more of these concepts. For example, the same historical phenomenon may be "feudal" in some aspects, "patrimonial" in others, "bureaucratic" in still others, and "charismatic" in still others. In order to ensure that these terms have an unambiguous meaning, sociology, for its part, must conceive of "pure" ("ideal") types of entities of this kind, each of which exhibits as complete a unity of meaning as possible. For this very reason, however, these types can never occur in reality in this absolutely ideal form, any more than a physical reaction calculated under the hypothesis of an absolute vacuum. Only from the pure ("ideal") type is sociological casuistry possible. It goes without saying that sociology, depending on the circumstances, also uses average types of an empirical-statistical nature, which do not require any particular methodological comment. However, when we speak of "typical" cases, we should understand by default the ideal type, which can be rational or irrational, mostly (in economic theory, for example, always) rational, but always constructed to be meaningfully adequate. It must be understood that, in the sociological field, "averages" and thus "average types" can be formed in a relatively unambiguous way only when they refer to variations in degree of qualitatively similar, meaningfully oriented action. Such cases do occur, but in the majority of cases, historically or sociologically relevant action is

influenced by qualitatively heterogeneous motives, among which it is not possible to establish an "average" in the proper sense. The ideal-typical constructions of social action used, for example, in economic theory are therefore "unrealistic" in the sense that they ask how one would act in the case of ideal and thus purely economically oriented rationality. These constructions help to understand real action, which is at least partly determined by inhibitions of tradition, affects, mistakes, and the intervention of non-economic goals or considerations, so that we might recognize its true motives (1) insofar as it is actually determined by rational economic purpose in the concrete case, or, on average, tends to be so, (2) but also precisely by the distance between its actual course of action and the ideal type. An ideal-type construction of a consistent mystical orientation towards life (e.g., towards politics and economics) should proceed in a similar way. The sharper and more unambiguous the ideal types are constructed, the more they deviate from reality, the better they serve both terminologically and classificatory as well as heuristically. The concrete causal explanation of individual events by historical analysis does not proceed otherwise when, for instance, in attempting to explain the course of the 1866 campaign, it first (conceptually) determines (as it must do) how both Moltke and Benedek would have acted in the case of ideal rationality, with full knowledge of their own situation and that of their enemy. It then compares how they acted in reality and causally explains the observed discrepancy (whether it is due to misinformation, actual error, error in reasoning, personal temperament, or considerations independent of strategy). Again, an ideal-typical construct of purposive rational action is used (implicitly).

The conceptual constructions of sociology are ideal types not only from an objective point of view but also in their application to subjective processes. In the vast majority of cases, actual action takes place in a state of muted semi-consciousness or unconsciousness of its "intended meaning". The actor "feels" this meaning more vaguely than he knows or "understands" it; in most cases, he acts on impulse or out of habit. Only occasionally is a meaning brought to consciousness (whether rational or irrational), and in the similar action of large numbers, it often applies only to a few individuals. Action that is truly meaningful, that is, fully conscious and clear, is in reality only a borderline case. Any historical or sociological analysis of reality must take this fact into account. But this should not prevent sociology from forming its concepts on the basis of a classification of possible types of "intended meanings," as if the action were actually consciously oriented towards meaning. The resulting deviation from concrete reality must always be taken into account, and its degree and nature determined.

On the methodological level, there is often a choice between unclear and clear, but then unreal and "ideal-typical" terms. In this case, however, the latter are scientifically preferable. (See Arch. f. Sozialwiss. XIX op. cit.)[12].

5.2 The concept of social action

1) Social action, including acts of omission or forbearance, can be directed towards past, present, or anticipated behavior of others (e.g., revenge for a past aggression, defense against present aggression, defense against future aggression). The "others" may be either individual persons and acquaintances or may constitute an indefinite plurality of completely unknown individuals ("money," for example, is a commodity that agents accept as payment because they base their actions on the expectation that a large but indefinite number of unknown individuals will be willing to accept it in exchange in the future).

2) Not every type of action, even if overt, qualifies as a "social action" in the sense used here. An overt action is not social if it is solely oriented towards the behavior of inanimate objects. Inner behavior is considered a social action only if it is oriented towards the behavior of others. For example, religious behavior is not social if it remains confined to contemplation or solitary prayer. The economic activity of an individual is considered social only to the extent that it takes into account the behavior of others. It is already social, in a general and formal sense, when it reflects respect for the de facto control of economic goods by others. Specifically, it becomes social when, for example, it takes into account the future needs of others in its consumption and directs its own "savings" toward them, or when it directs its production toward the future needs of others, and so on.

3) Not every type of interaction between individuals is social. It is social only when one's behavior is meaningfully oriented toward the behavior of others. For example, a collision between two cyclists is a mere event, just like a natural occurrence. However, their attempts to avoid each other, along with any subsequent insults, fights, or peaceful discussions following the collision, would constitute social actions.

4) Social action is neither the uniform action of several people nor any action influenced by the behavior of others.

a) If a crowd of people on the street simultaneously open their umbrellas at the start of rain, the action of one individual is not typically directed by that of another. Rather, all actions are uniformly oriented towards the shared need for protection from the rain.

b) It is well known that the action of individuals is strongly influenced by the mere fact that they find themselves within a crowd at a certain location (this is the subject matter of "crowd psychology" studies, such as those of Le Bon). This phenomenon can be called "mass action." Even the behavior of a large number of dispersed individuals can become mass-conditioned, and perceived as such, through the simultaneous or sequential actions of several of them (for example, through the channel of the press). The simple fact of feeling part of a crowd can enable certain types of reactions and hinder others. Hence, a particular event or human behavior can trigger the most diverse feelings – exhilaration, anger, enthusiasm, despair, and passions of all kinds – that might not occur (or not as easily) if the individuals were isolated, without there being (in many instances at least) a meaningful relationship between their situation and that of the crowd. Action that is reactively prompted or influenced by the mere presence of a crowd, without any meaningful connection to it, would not be "social" in the sense we understand it here. Of course, the distinction is quite fluid. The degree of meaningful connection to the phenomenon of the "mass" can be variable and open to different interpretations, as we see in the case of demagogues and often in the case of the mass public itself.

Moreover, the mere "imitation" of the action of others (the importance of which G. Tarde rightly emphasized) would not be conceptually "social action" if it were merely reactive, without any meaningful orientation to that of others. The boundary is so fluid that it is often difficult to make a distinction. However, the mere fact that someone adopts a procedure that seems appropriate to him and that he has learned from others is not social action in the sense that we understand it. This action is not oriented to the actions of others, but rather to the understanding of certain objective possibilities that the actor has become aware of through observation. His action is thus causally determined by the actions of others, but not meaningfully. Conversely, if the actor imitates another's action because it is "fashionable," because it is considered traditional, exemplary, or "distinguished," or for other similar reasons, it is a meaningful relationship, oriented either toward the behavior of the imitated or toward that of third parties, or both. Of course, there are all sorts of gradations in between. The two cases of mass behavior and imitation are floating and represent borderline cases of social action, a concept we will often return to, for example, in the context of traditional action (§2). In this case, as in others, the reason for the indeterminacy lies in the fact that both the orientation toward the behavior of others and the meaning of one's own action are not always clearly identifiable, nor even conscious, let alone fully conscious. For this reason, mere "influence" and meaningful "orientation" cannot always be distinguished with certainty. But conceptually, they should be separated, although of course "reactive" imitation has at least the same sociological significance as "social action" in the proper sense. Sociology is by no means exclusively concerned with "social action," but for the kind of sociology we are discussing here, it is its central fact, the one that is, so to speak, constitutive of it as a science. This in no way implies any judgment about the relative importance of this fact compared to others.

5.2.1 Types of social action

§ In terms of its orientation, social action, like any action, can be:

1.   Instrumentally rational [zweckrational]: Guided by expectations of the behavior of objects in the external world and of other people, using these expectations as "conditions" or "means" to achieve one's own rationally pursued and evaluated ends.
2.   Value-rational [wertrational]: Driven by a conscious belief in the unconditional and intrinsic value – be it ethical, aesthetic, religious, or otherwise – of a specific self-conduct, valued purely for its own sake, irrespective of its outcome.
3.   Affective, especially emotional: Influenced by current affects and emotional states.
4.   Traditional: Stemming from a well-established habit.

1) Strictly traditional behavior, like the purely reactive imitation previously mentioned, is completely on the borderline and often beyond what can be called "meaningfully" oriented action. For it is often only a blind reaction to habitual stimuli, following the course of an already-experienced pattern of behavior. The vast majority of everyday actions come close to this type. However, its place in a typology is not simply as a borderline case, since, as we will show later, the attachment to habitual patterns can be consciously maintained to varying degrees and in different directions, in which case this type comes close to that of value rationality.

2) Purely affective behavior is also on the borderline and often goes beyond what is consciously "meaningful"; it may consist of an uncontrolled reaction to an extraordinary stimulus. It is a case of sublimation when the action, conditioned by the affect, serves as a conscious release of the emotional state. It is then usually (but not always) on the way to value-rational or instrumentally rational action, or both.

3) Affective and value-rational orientation of action differ in that the latter consciously determines the ultimate direction of action and consistently orients itself toward it in a planned manner. Otherwise, they have in common that the meaning of the action does not lie in the outcome beyond it but in the performance of the action itself. Those who act affectively satisfy their present needs for revenge, pleasure, devotion, contemplative bliss, or reaction to present affects (whether ordinary or sublime). Those who act purely rationally in value are those who, without regard to foreseeable consequences, act in the service of their belief in duty, dignity, beauty, religious doctrine, piety, or the importance of a "cause," whatever it may be. Value-rational action always conforms to the "commandments" or "requirements" that the actors believe to be binding upon them. It is only when human action is guided by such imperatives that it is said to be value-rational, which happens only in a very variable fraction of cases, usually quite modest. As we will see, it is significant enough to be singled out as a special type, even though we are not trying to provide an exhaustive classification of types of action here.

4) Instrumentally rational action is oriented towards ends, means, and secondary consequences. In this type of action, means are rationally weighed against ends, ends are evaluated against secondary consequences, and, finally, the various possible ends are compared with each other; thus, in all cases, action is not affectively (and especially not emotionally) or traditionally oriented. The choice between competing and conflicting ends and consequences may well be value-rational. Then the action is rational only in its means. Alternatively, without a value-rational orientation, actors may simply rank competing and conflicting ends as given subjective wants on a scale of urgency that they consciously weigh, and orient their action according to this scale in such a way that they are satisfied in this order as far as possible ("principle of marginal utility"). Thus, value-rational action can hold various relationships to instrumentally rational action. From the point of view of instrumental rationality, however, value-rational action is always irrational, and all the more so because it gives a more absolute meaning to the value that orients the action, because it reflects the consequences of the action all the less, since it is directed unconditionally according to its intrinsic value (purity of spirit, beauty, absolute goodness, absolute duty). Absolute instrumental rationality of action, however, is also only an essentially hypothetical borderline case.

5) Action, especially social action, is very rarely oriented in only one of these directions. Likewise, these types of orientations do not encompass all possible types of action orientation but rather represent conceptually pure types constructed for sociological purposes, to which real action more or less approximates, or of which it is, in most cases, a mixture. Their usefulness to us can only result from their fruitfulness.

5.2.2 The concept of social relationship

§ Social "relationship" shall refer to a mutually adjusted and thereby meaningfully oriented behavior of several individuals. Thus, the social relation consists entirely and exclusively in the possibility of a meaningful orientation of action, whatever the basis of this possibility may be for the time being.

1) A fundamental characteristic of the concept shall therefore be the existence of a minimum degree of mutual orientation of the action of each to that of others. Its content can be of the most varied nature: Fight, hostility, sexual attraction, friendship, piety, commercial exchange, "fulfillment," "circumvention" or "rupture" of an agreement, economic, erotic, or other "competition," corporate, national, or class groups (provided that they lead to social action beyond simple commonalities, which will be discussed later). Hence, the definition does not say whether there is "solidarity" between the actors or the reverse.

2) The meaning that orients individual actions is always that which is aimed at by the actors in a particular concrete case, on average, or in the

"pure" type constructed; it never refers to a normatively "correct" or meta-physically "true" meaning. The social relationship consists exclusively and solely in the possibility that an action in a specifiable way appropriate to this meaning is occurring or will occur, even when it is about so-called "social structures" [soziale Gebilde] such as the "state," the "church," the "cooperative," the "marriage," and so on. We must always keep this in mind in order to avoid a "substantial" understanding of these concepts. For example, a "state" ceases to "exist" sociologically when there is no longer any potential for certain types of meaningfully-oriented social action to occur. This potential may be significant or negligible. However, in any case, it is only to the extent that it has existed or does exist (according to the estimation) that the corresponding social relationship existed or exists. It is not possible to give a more precise meaning to the statement that, for example, a certain "state" still exists or no longer exists.

3) It is by no means said that all the actors involved in a given social relationship attribute the same subjective meaning to it or that they position themselves internally according to the attitude of the other party. There is not always "reciprocity" in this sense. "Friendship," "love," "piety," "faithfulness to the contract," "patriotism" on one side can be confronted with completely different attitudes on the other. The actors then attach a different meaning to their actions, and the social relationship is objectively "asymmetrical" from the point of view of the parties. However, it is also reciprocal in the sense that the actors assume (even if partially or completely wrongly) a certain attitude of their partners towards them and direct their own actions according to these expectations, which can and usually will have consequences for the course of action and the shaping of the relationship. A relationship is objectively "reciprocal" only to the extent that the meanings "correspond" to each other according to the average expectations of each of the actors, for example, in the case where the children's attitude toward the father at least approximately corresponds to the father's expectations (in the individual case, on average, or typically). In reality, a social relationship based entirely on reciprocal attitudes is only a marginal case. However, according to our terminology, the absence of reciprocity should only preclude the existence of a "social relationship" if it leads to the effective absence of a mutual relationship between the actions of the two parties. Here, as elsewhere in reality, all kinds of transitions are the rule.

4) A social relationship can be either totally transitory or durable, that is, established in such a way that there is a chance of recurrence of a given significant behavior, which is therefore expected accordingly. To avoid misunderstandings, it must always be kept in mind that it is only the presence of this possibility – the greater or lesser chance that a meaningful action will occur – that underpins the "existence" of the social relationship. That a "friendship" or a "state of affairs" exists or has existed therefore means exclusively

and solely that we (the observers) judge that there is or has been a possibility that, on the basis of certain known subjective attitudes of certain individuals, a certain specific type of action will occur on average and nothing else. The unavoidable question in legal reasoning – that is, whether a law is valid or not (in the legal sense), and thus whether a legal relationship "exists" or not – has no value in sociology.

5) The meaning of a social relationship can vary. For example, a political relationship can change from solidarity to conflict of interest. Whether we say that a "new" relationship has been established or that the existing old relationship has acquired a new "meaning" is simply a matter of terminological convenience and the degree of continuity in the change. Moreover, meaning can be partly perennial and partly variable.

6) The meaningful content that grounds a social relationship in a long-term manner can be formulated in "maxims" that the participants expect their partner(s) to respect on average and approximately, and on which they orient their actions (on average and approximately). This is especially true if the action in question is (in relation to values or to given ends) rational. In the case of an erotic or emotional relationship (e.g., a relationship of "piety"), the potential for rational formulation of the intended meaning is naturally much less than in the case of, for example, a contractual relationship of a commercial nature.

7) The meaning of a social relationship may be agreed upon by mutual commitment. This means that the parties involved in it make promises about their future behavior (either to each other or in some other way). All participants then rely, as far as they rationally consider things, on the fact that the others will orient their action according to the meaning of the agreement as they themselves understand it. They orient their own action according to this expectation, partly instrumentally rationally (depending on the case, with varying degrees of subjectively "loyal" intentions on their part) and partly value-rationally, driven by a sense of the "duty" to uphold their side of the agreement as they understand it. We will leave the discussion here for now. For further details, please refer to sections § 9 and § 13.

Notes

1 Weber, M. (1922). *Wirtschaft und Gesellschaft [Economy and society]* (pp. 1–14). Tübingen: Mohr Siebeck.
2 Translator's note: See Weber (1913).
3 Translator's note: See Jaspers (1913).
4 Translator's note: See Rickert (1896/1902).
5 Translator's note: See Simmel (1905).
6 Translator's note: See Gottl (1901).
7 Translator's note: See Tönnies (1887).
8 Translator's note: See Stammler (1896).
9 Translator's note: See Weber (1907).

10 Translator's note: See Simmel (1908).
11 Translator's note: See Simmel (1900).
12 Translator's note: See Weber (1907).

References

Escherich, K. (1909). *Die Termiten oder weissen Ameisen* [The Termites or White Ants]. Leipzig: W Klinkhardt.

Gottl, F. (1901). *Die Herrschaft des Wortes [The rule of the word]*. Jena: Fisher.

Jaspers, K. (1913). *Allgemeine Psychopathologie [General psychopathology]*. Berlin: Springer.

Rickert, H. (1896/1902). *Grenzen der naturwissenschaftlichen Begriffsbildung. Begriffsbildung [Limits to the formation of concepts in the natural sciences]* (2nd ed.). Tübingen: J.C.B. Mohr.

Schäffle, A. (1881). *Bau und Leben des sozialen Körpers.* [Construction and Life of the Social Body]. Tubingen: H. Laupp.

Simmel, G. (1900). *Philos. des Geldes [Philosophy of money]*. Leipzig: Duncker & Humblot.

Simmel, G. (1905). *Problemen der Geschichtsphilosophie [Problems of the philosophy of history]*. Leipzig: Verlag von Duncker& Humblot.

Simmel, G. (1908). *Soziologie: Untersuchungen über die Formen der Vergesellschaftung [Sociology: Inquiries into the construction of social forms]*. Berlin: Duncker & Humblot.

Stammler, R. (1896). *Wirtschaft und Recht nach der materialistischen Geschichtsauffassung [Economy and law according to the materialist conception of history]*. Leipzig: Veit & Comp.

Tönnies, F. (1887). *Gemeinschaft und Gesellschaft [Community and society]*. Leipzig: Verlag.

Weber, M. (1907). Rudolf Stammlers Überwindung der materialistischen Geschichtsauffassung [Rudolf Stammler's overcoming of the materialistic conception of history]. *Archiv f. Sozialwissensch, xxiv*, 94–151.

Weber, M. (1913). Über einige Kategorien der verstehenden Soziologie [About some categories of understanding sociology]. *Logos, iv*, 253–294.

Index

For Product Safety Concerns and Information please contact our EU
representative GPSR@taylorandfrancis.com
Taylor & Francis Verlag GmbH, Kaufingerstraße 24, 80331 München, Germany

www.ingramcontent.com/pod-product-compliance
Lightning Source LLC
Chambersburg PA
CBHW050538270326
41926CB00015B/3279

9 7 8 1 0 3 2 6 2 7 0 3 8